The Book
of American
Negro Poetry

The Book of American Negro Poetry

James Weldon Johnson

MINT EDITIONS

The Book of American Negro Poetry was first published in 1922.

This edition published by Mint Editions 2021.

ISBN 9781513282404 | E-ISBN 9781513287423

Published by Mint Editions®

 MINT EDITIONS

minteditionbooks.com

Publishing Director: Jennifer Newens
Design & Production: Rachel Lopez Metzger
Project Manager: Micaela Clark
Typesetting: Westchester Publishing Services

Contents

JOSEPH S. COTTER, JR.

ROSCOE C. JAMISON

JESSIE FAUSET

ANNE SPENCER

PREFACE

There is, perhaps, a better excuse for giving an Anthology of American Negro Poetry to the public than can be offered for many of the anthologies that have recently been issued. The public, generally speaking, does not know that there are American Negro poets—to supply this lack of information is, alone, a work worthy of somebody's effort.

Moreover, the matter of Negro poets and the production of literature by the colored people in this country involves more than supplying information that is lacking. It is a matter which has a direct bearing on the most vital of American problems.

A people may become great through many means, but there is only one measure by which its greatness is recognized and acknowledged. The final measure of the greatness of all peoples is the amount and standard of the literature and art they have produced. The world does not know that a people is great until that people produces great literature and art. No people that has produced great literature and art has ever been looked upon by the world as distinctly inferior.

The status of the Negro in the United States' is more a question of national mental attitude toward the race than of actual conditions. And nothing will do more to change that mental attitude and raise his status than a demonstration of intellectual parity by the Negro through the production of literature and art.

Is there likelihood that the American Negro will be able to do this? There is, for the good reason that he possesses the innate powers. He has the emotional endowment, the originality and artistic conception, and, what is more important, the power of creating that which has universal appeal and influence.

I make here what may appear to be a more startling statement by saying that the Negro has already proved the possession of these powers by being the creator of the only things artistic that have yet sprung from American soil and been universally acknowledged as distinctive American products.

These creations by the American Negro may be summed up under four heads. The first two are the Uncle Remus stories, which were collected by Joel Chandler Harris, and the "spirituals" or slave songs, to which the Fisk Jubilee Singers made the public and the musicians of both the United States and Europe listen. The Uncle Remus stories constitute the greatest body of folklore that America has produced, and the "spirituals" the greatest body of folk-song. I shall speak of the "spirituals" later because they are more than folk-songs, for in them the Negro sounded the depths, if he did not scale the heights, of music.

The other two creations are the Cakewalk and ragtime. We do not need to go very far back to remember when cakewalking was the rage in the United States, Europe and South America. Society in this country and royalty abroad spent time in practicing the intricate steps. Paris pronounced it the "poetry of motion." The popularity of the cakewalk passed away but its influence remained. The influence can be seen to-day on any American stage where there is dancing.

The influence which the Negro has exercised on the art of dancing in this country has been almost absolute. For generations the "buck and wing" and the "stop-time" dances, which are strictly Negro, have been familiar to American theatre audiences. A few years ago the public discovered the "turkey trot," the "eagle rock," "ballin' the jack," and several other varieties that started the modern dance craze. These dances were quickly followed by the "tango," a dance originated by the Negroes of Cuba and later transplanted to South America. (This fact is attested by no less authority than Vincente Blasco Ibañez in his "Four Horsemen of the Apocalypse.") Half the floor space in the country was then turned over to dancing, and highly paid exponents sprang up everywhere. The most noted, Mr. Vernon Castle, and, by the way, an Englishman, never danced except to the music of a colored band, and he never failed to state to his audiences that most of his dances had long been done by "your colored people," as he put it.

Any one who witnesses a musical production in which there is dancing cannot fail to notice the Negro stamp on all the movements; a stamp which even the great vogue of Russian dances that swept the country about the time of the popular dance craze could not affect. That peculiar swaying of the shoulders which you see done everywhere by the blond girls of the chorus is nothing more than a movement from the Negro dance referred to above, the "eagle rock." Occasionally the movement takes on a suggestion of the, now outlawed, "shimmy."

As for Ragtime, I go straight to the statement that it is the one artistic production by which America is known the world over. It has been all-conquering. Everywhere it is hailed as "American music."

JAMES WELDON JOHNSON

For a dozen years or so there has been a steady tendency to divorce Ragtime from the Negro; in fact, to take from him the credit of having originated it. Probably the younger people of the present generation do not know that Ragtime is of Negro origin. The change wrought in Ragtime and the way in which it is accepted by the country have been brought about chiefly through the change which has gradually been made in the words and stories accompanying the music. Once the text of all Ragtime songs was written in Negro dialect, and was about Negroes in the cabin or in the cotton field or on the levee or at a jubilee or on Sixth Avenue or at a ball, and about their love affairs. To-day, only a small proportion of Ragtime songs relate at all to the Negro. The truth is, Ragtime is now national rather than racial. But that does not abolish in any way the claim of the American Negro as its originator.

Ragtime music was originated by colored piano players in the questionable resorts of St. Louis, Memphis, and other Mississippi River towns. These men did not know any more about the theory of music than they did about the theory of the universe. They were guided by their natural musical instinct and talent, but above all by the Negro's extraordinary sense of rhythm. Any one who is familiar with Ragtime may note that its chief charm is not in melody, but in rhythms. These players often improvised crude and, at times, vulgar words to fit the music. This was the beginning of the Ragtime song.

Ragtime music got its first popular hearing at Chicago during the world's fair in that city. From Chicago it made its way to New York, and then started on its universal triumph.

The earliest Ragtime songs, like Topsy, "jes' grew." Some of these earliest songs were taken down by white men, the words slightly altered or changed, and published under the names of the arrangers. They sprang into immediate popularity and earned small fortunes. The first to become widely known was "The Bully," a levee song which had been long used by roustabouts along the Mississippi. It was introduced in New York by Miss May Irwin, and gained instant popularity. Another one of these "jes' grew" songs was one which for a while disputed for place with Yankee Doodle; perhaps, disputes it even to-day. That song was "A Hot Time in the Old Town To-night"; introduced and made popular by the colored regimental bands during the Spanish-American War.

Later there came along a number of colored men who were able to transcribe the old songs and write original ones. I was, about that time, writing words to music for the music show stage in New York. I was collaborating with my brother, J. Rosamond Johnson, and the late Bob Cole. I remember that we appropriated about the last one of the old "jes' grew" songs. It was a song which had been sung for years all through the South. The words were unprintable, but the tune was irresistible, and belonged to nobody. We took it, re-wrote the verses, telling an entirely different story from the original, left the chorus as it was, and published the song, at first under the name of "Will Handy." It became very popular with college boys, especially at football games, and perhaps still is. The song was, "Oh, Didn't He Ramble!"

In the beginning, and for quite a while, almost all of the Ragtime songs that were deliberately composed were the work of colored writers. Now, the colored composers, even in this particular field, are greatly outnumbered by the white.

The reader might be curious to know if the "jes' grew" songs have ceased to grow. No, they have not; they are growing all the time. The country has lately been flooded with several varieties of "The Blues." These "Blues," too, had their origin in Memphis, and the towns along the Mississippi. They are a sort of lament of a lover who is feeling "blue" over the loss of his sweetheart. The "Blues" of Memphis have been adulterated so much on Broadway that they have lost their pristine hue. But whenever you hear a piece of music which has a strain like this in it: you will know you are listening to something which belonged originally to Beale Avenue, Memphis, Tennessee. The original "Memphis Blues," so far as it can be credited to a composer, must be credited to Mr. W. C. Handy, a colored musician of Memphis.

As illustrations of the genuine Ragtime song in the making, I quote the words of two that were popular with the Southern colored soldiers in France. Here is the first:

"Mah mammy's lyin' in her grave,
Mah daddy done run away,
Mah sister's married a gamblin' man,
An' I've done gone astray.
Yes, I've done gone astray, po' boy,
An' I've done gone astray,
Mah sister's married a gamblin' man,
An' I've done gone astray, po' boy."

These lines are crude, but they contain something of real poetry, of that elusive thing which nobody can define and that you can only tell that it is there when you feel it. You cannot read these lines without becoming reflective and feeling sorry for "Po' Boy."

Now, take in this word picture of utter dejection:

> *"I'm jes' as misabul as I can be,*
> *I'm unhappy even if I am free,*
> *I'm feelin' down, I'm feelin' blue;*
> *I wander 'round, don't know what to do.*
> *I'm go'n lay mah haid on de railroad line,*
> *Let de B. & O. come and pacify mah min'."*

These lines are, no doubt, one of the many versions of the famous "Blues." They are also crude, but they go straight to the mark. The last two lines move with the swiftness of all great tragedy.

In spite of the bans which musicians and music teachers have placed on it, the people still demand and enjoy Ragtime. In fact, there is not a corner of the civilized world in which it is not known and liked. And this proves its originality, for if it were an imitation, the people of Europe, at least, would not have found it a novelty. And it is proof of a more important thing, it is proof that Ragtime possesses the vital spark, the power to appeal universally, without which any artistic production, no matter how approved its form may be, is dead.

Of course, there are those who will deny that Ragtime is an artistic production. American musicians, especially, instead of investigating Ragtime, dismiss it with a contemptuous word. But this has been the course of scholasticism in every branch of art. Whatever new thing the people like is pooh-poohed; whatever is popular is regarded as not worth while. The fact is, nothing great or enduring in music has ever sprung full-fledged from the brain of any master; the best he gives the world he gathers from the hearts of the people, and runs it through the alembic of his genius.

Ragtime deserves serious attention. There is a lot of colorless and vicious imitation, but there is enough that is genuine. In one composition alone, "The Memphis Blues," the musician will find not only great melodic beauty, but a polyphonic structure that is amazing.

It is obvious that Ragtime has influenced, and in a large measure, become our popular music; but not many would know that it has influenced even our religious music. Those who are familiar with gospel hymns can at once see this influence if they will compare the songs of thirty years ago, such as "In the Sweet Bye and Bye," "The Ninety and Nine," etc., with the up-to-date, syncopated tunes that are sung in Sunday Schools, Christian Endeavor Societies, Y.M.C.A.'s and like gatherings to-day.

Ragtime has not only influenced American music, it has influenced American life; indeed, it has saturated American life. It has become the popular medium for our national expression musically. And who can say that it does not express the blare and jangle and the surge, too, of our national spirit?

Any one who doubts that there is a peculiar heel-tickling, smile-provoking, joy-awakening, response-compelling charm in Ragtime needs only to hear a skilful performer play the genuine article, needs only to listen to its bizarre harmonies, its audacious resolutions often consisting of an abrupt jump from one key to another, its intricate rhythms in which the accents fall in the most unexpected places but in which the fundamental beat is never lost in order to be convinced. I believe it has its place as well as the music which draws from us sighs and tears.

Now, these dances which I have referred to and Ragtime music may be lower forms of art, but they are evidence of a power that will some day be applied to the higher forms. And even now we need not stop at the Negro's accomplishment through these lower forms. In the "spirituals," or slave songs, the Negro has given America not only its only folksongs, but a mass of noble music. I never think of this music but that I am struck by the wonder, the miracle of its production. How did the men who originated these songs manage to do it? The sentiments are easily accounted for; they are, for the most part, taken from the Bible. But the melodies, where did they come from? Some of them so weirdly sweet, and others so wonderfully strong. Take, for instance, "Go Down, Moses"; I doubt that there is a stronger theme in the whole musical literature of the world.

It is to be noted that whereas the chief characteristic of Ragtime is rhythm, the chief characteristic of the "spirituals" is melody. The melodies of "Steal Away to Jesus," "Swing Low Sweet Chariot," "Nobody Knows de Trouble I See," "I Couldn't Hear Nobody Pray," "Deep River," "O, Freedom Over Me," and many others of these songs possess a beauty that is—what shall I say? poignant. In the riotous rhythms of Ragtime the Negro expressed his irrepressible buoyancy, his keen response to the sheer joy of living; in the "spirituals" he voiced his sense of beauty and his deep religious feeling.

Naturally, not as much can be said for the words of these songs as for the music. Most of the songs are religious. Some of them are songs expressing faith and endurance and a longing for freedom. In the religious songs, the sentiments and often the entire lines are taken bodily from the Bible. However, there is no doubt that some of these religious songs have a meaning apart from the Biblical text. It is evident that the opening lines of "Go Down, Moses,"

> *"Go down, Moses,*
> *'Way down in Egypt land;*
> *Tell old Pharoah,*
> *Let my people go."*

have a significance beyond the bondage of Israel in Egypt.

The bulk of the lines to these songs, as is the case in all communal music, is made up of choral iteration and incremental repetition of the leader's lines. If the words are read, this constant iteration and repetition are found to be tiresome; and it must be admitted that the lines themselves are often very trite. And, yet, there is frequently revealed a flash of real, primitive poetry. I give the following examples:

> *"Sometimes I feel like an eagle in de air."*

> *"You may bury me in de East,*
> *You may bury me in de West,*
> *But I'll hear de trumpet sound*
> *In-a dat mornin'."*

> *"I know de moonlight, I know de starlight;*
> *I lay dis body down.*
> *I walk in de moonlight, I walk in de starlight;*
> *I lay dis body down.*
> *I know de graveyard, I know de graveyard,*
> *When I lay dis body down.*
> *I walk in de graveyard, I walk troo de graveyard*
> *To lay dis body down.*

I lay in de grave an' stretch out my arms;
I lay dis body down.
I go to de judgment in de evenin' of de day
When I lay dis body down.
An' my soul an' yo' soul will meet in de day
When I lay dis body down."

Regarding the line, "I lay in de grave an' stretch out my arms," Col. Thomas Wentworth Higginson of Boston, one of the first to give these slave songs serious study, said: "Never it seems to me, since man first lived and suffered, was his infinite longing for peace uttered more plaintively than in that line."

These Negro folksongs constitute a vast mine of material that has been neglected almost absolutely. The only white writers who have in recent years given adequate attention and study to this music, that I know of, are Mr. H.E. Krehbiel and Mrs. Natalie Curtis Burlin. We have our native composers denying the worth and importance of this music, and trying to manufacture grand opera out of so-called Indian themes.

But there is a great hope for the development of this music, and that hope is the Negro himself. A worthy beginning has already been made by Burleigh, Cook, Johnson, and Dett. And there will yet come great Negro composers who will take this music and voice through it not only the soul of their race, but the soul of America.

And does it not seem odd that this greatest gift of the Negro has been the most neglected of all he possesses? Money and effort have been expended upon his development in every direction except this. This gift has been regarded as a kind of side show, something for occasional exhibition; wherein it is the touchstone, it is the magic thing, it is that by which the Negro can bridge all chasms. No persons, however hostile, can listen to Negroes singing this wonderful music without having their hostility melted down.

This power of the Negro to suck up the national spirit from the soil and create something artistic and original, which, at the same time, possesses the note of universal appeal, is due to a remarkable racial gift of adaptability; it is more than adaptability, it is a transfusive quality. And the Negro has exercised this transfusive quality not only here in America, where the race lives in large numbers, but in European countries, where the number has been almost infinitesimal.

Is it not curious to know that the greatest poet of Russia is Alexander

Pushkin, a man of African descent; that the greatest romancer of France is Alexander Dumas, a man of African descent; and that one of the greatest musicians of England is Coleridge-Taylor, a man of African descent?

The fact is fairly well known that the father of Dumas was a Negro of the French West Indies, and that the father of Coleridge-Taylor was a native-born African; but the facts concerning Pushkin's African ancestry are not so familiar.

When Peter the Great was Czar of Russia, some potentate presented him with a full-blooded Negro of gigantic size. Peter, the most eccentric ruler of modern times, dressed this Negro up in soldier clothes, christened him Hannibal, and made him a special body-guard.

But Hannibal had more than size, he had brain and ability. He not only looked picturesque and imposing in soldier clothes, he showed that he had in him the making of a real soldier. Peter recognized this, and eventually made him a general. He afterwards ennobled him, and Hannibal, later, married one of the ladies of the Russian court. This same Hannibal was great-grandfather of Pushkin, the national poet of Russia, the man who bears the same relation to Russian literature that Shakespeare bears to English literature.

I know the question naturally arises: If out of the few Negroes who have lived in France there came a Dumas; and out of the few Negroes who have lived in England there came a Coleridge-Taylor; and if from the man who was at the time, probably, the only Negro in Russia there sprang that country's national poet, why have not the millions of Negroes in the United States with all the emotional and artistic endowment claimed for them produced a Dumas, or a Coleridge-Taylor, or a Pushkin?

The question seems difficult, but there is an answer. The Negro in the United States is consuming all of his intellectual energy in this gruelling race-struggle. And the same statement may be made in a general way about the white South. Why does not the white South produce literature and art? The white South, too, is consuming all of its intellectual energy in this lamentable conflict. Nearly all of the mental efforts of the white South run through one narrow channel. The life of every Southern white man and all of his activities are impassably limited by the ever present Negro problem. And that is why, as Mr. H. L. Mencken puts it, in all that vast region, with its thirty or forty million people and its territory as large as a half a dozen Frances or Germanys, there is not a single poet, not a serious historian, not a creditable composer, not a critic good or bad, not a dramatist dead or alive.

But, even so, the American Negro has accomplished something in pure literature. The list of those who have done so would be surprising both by its length and the excellence of the achievements. One of the great books written in this country since the Civil War is the work of a colored man, "The Souls of Black Folk," by W.E.B. Du Bois.

Such a list begins with Phillis Wheatley. In 1761 a slave ship landed a cargo of slaves in Boston. Among them was a little girl seven or eight years of age. She attracted the attention of John Wheatley, a wealthy gentleman of Boston, who purchased her as a servant for his wife. Mrs. Wheatley was a benevolent woman. She noticed the girl's quick mind and determined to give her opportunity for its development. Twelve years later Phillis published a volume of poems. The book was brought out in London, where Phillis was for several months an object of great curiosity and attention.

Phillis Wheatley has never been given her rightful place in American literature. By some sort of conspiracy she is kept out of most of the books, especially the text-books on literature used in the schools. Of course, she is not a *great* American poet—and in her day there were no great American poets—but she is an important American poet. Her importance, if for no other reason, rests on the fact that, save one, she is the first in order of time of all the women poets of America. And she is among the first of all American poets to issue a volume.

It seems strange that the books generally give space to a mention of Urian Oakes, President of Harvard College, and to quotations from the crude and lengthy elegy which he published in 1667; and print examples from the execrable versified version of the Psalms made by the New England divines, and yet deny a place to Phillis Wheatley.

Here are the opening lines from the elegy by Oakes, which is quoted from in most of the books on American literature:

> *"Reader, I am no poet, but I grieve.*
> *Behold here what that passion can do,*
> *That forced a verse without Apollo's leave,*
> *And whether the learned sisters would or no."*

There was no need for Urian to admit what his handiwork declared. But this from the versified Psalms is still worse, yet it is found in the books:

> *"The Lord's song sing can we? being*
> *in stranger's land, then let*
> *lose her skill my right hand if I*
> *Jerusalem forget."*

Anne Bradstreet preceded Phillis Wheatley by a little over twenty years. She published her volume of poems, "The Tenth Muse," in 1750. Let us strike a comparison between the two. Anne Bradstreet was a wealthy, cultivated Puritan girl, the daughter of Thomas Dudley, Governor of Bay Colony. Phillis, as we know, was a Negro slave girl born in Africa. Let us take them both at their best and in the same vein. The following stanza is from Anne's poem entitled "Contemplation":

> *"While musing thus with contemplation fed,*
> *And thousand fancies buzzing in my brain,*
> *The sweet tongued Philomel percht o'er my head,*
> *And chanted forth a most melodious strain,*
> *Which rapt me so with wonder and delight,*
> *I judged my hearing better than my sight,*
> *And wisht me wings with her awhile to take my flight."*

And the following is from Phillis' poem entitled "Imagination":

> *"Imagination! who can sing thy force?*
> *Or who describe the swiftness of thy course?*
> *Soaring through air to find the bright abode,*
> *The empyreal palace of the thundering God,*
> *We on thy pinions can surpass the wind,*
> *And leave the rolling universe behind,*
> *From star to star the mental optics rove,*
> *Measure the skies, and range the realms above,*
> *There in one view we grasp the mighty whole,*
> *Or with new worlds amaze the unbounded soul."*

We do not think the black woman suffers much by comparison with the white. Thomas Jefferson said of Phillis: "Religion has produced a Phillis Wheatley, but it could not produce a poet; her poems are beneath contempt." It is quite likely that Jefferson's criticism was directed more against religion than against Phillis' poetry. On the other hand, General

George Washington wrote her with his own hand a letter in which he thanked her for a poem which she had dedicated to him. He, later, received her with marked courtesy at his camp at Cambridge.

It appears certain that Phillis was the first person to apply to George Washington the phrase, "First in peace." The phrase occurs in her poem addressed to "His Excellency, General George Washington," written in 1775. The encomium, "First in war, first in peace, first in the hearts of his countrymen" was originally used in the resolutions presented to Congress on the death of Washington, December, 1799.

Phillis Wheatley's poetry is the poetry of the Eighteenth Century. She wrote when Pope and Gray were supreme; it is easy to see that Pope was her model. Had she come under the influence of Wordsworth, Byron or Keats or Shelley, she would have done greater work. As it is, her work must not be judged by the work and standards of a later day, but by the work and standards of her own day and her own contemporaries. By this method of criticism she stands out as one of the important characters in the making of American literature, without any allowances for her sex or her antecedents.

According to "A Bibliographical Checklist of American Negro Poetry," compiled by Mr. Arthur A. Schomburg, more than one hundred Negroes in the United States have published volumes of poetry ranging in size from pamphlets to books of from one hundred to three hundred pages. About thirty of these writers fill in the gap between Phillis Wheatley and Paul Laurence Dunbar. Just here it is of interest to note that a Negro wrote and published a poem before Phillis Wheatley arrived in this country from Africa. He was Jupiter Hammon, a slave belonging to a Mr. Lloyd of Queens-Village, Long Island. In 1760 Hammon published a poem, eighty-eight lines in length, entitled "An Evening Thought, Salvation by Christ, with Penettential Cries." In 1788 he published "An Address to Miss Phillis Wheatley, Ethiopian Poetess in Boston, who came from Africa at eight years of age, and soon became acquainted with the Gospel of Jesus Christ." These two poems do not include all that Hammon wrote.

The poets between Phillis Wheatley and Dunbar must be considered more in the light of what they attempted than of what they accomplished. Many of them showed marked talent, but barely a half dozen of them demonstrated even mediocre mastery of technique in the use of poetic material and forms. And yet there are several names that deserve mention. George M. Horton, Frances E. Harper, James M. Bell and

Alberry A. Whitman, all merit consideration when due allowances are made for their limitations in education, training and general culture. The limitations of Horton were greater than those of either of the others; he was born a slave in North Carolina in 1797, and as a young man began to compose poetry without being able to write it down. Later he received some instruction from professors of the University of North Carolina, at which institution he was employed as a janitor. He published a volume of poems, "The Hope of Liberty," in 1829.

Mrs. Harper, Bell and Whitman would stand out if only for the reason that each of them attempted sustained work. Mrs. Harper published her first volume of poems in 1854, but later she published "Moses, a Story of the Nile," a poem which ran to 52 closely printed pages. Bell in 1864 published a poem of 28 pages in celebration of President Lincoln's Emancipation Proclamation. In 1870 he published a poem of 32 pages in celebration of the ratification of the Fifteenth Amendment to the Constitution. Whitman published his first volume of poems, a book of 253 pages, in 1877; but in 1884 he published "The Rape of Florida," an epic poem written in four cantos and done in the Spenserian stanza, and which ran to 97 closely printed pages. The poetry of both Mrs. Harper and of Whitman had a large degree of popularity; one of Mrs. Harper's books went through more than twenty editions.

Of these four poets, it is Whitman who reveals not only the greatest imagination but also the more skilful workmanship. His lyric power at its best may be judged from the following stanza from the "Rape of Florida":

> "*Come now, my love, the moon is on the lake;*
> *Upon the waters is my light canoe;*
> *Come with me, love, and gladsome oars shall make*
> *A music on the parting wave for you.*
> *Come o'er the waters deep and dark and blue;*
> *Come where the lilies in the marge have sprung,*
> *Come with me, love, for Oh, my love is true!'*
> *This is the song that on the lake was sung,*
> *The boatman sang it when his heart was young.*"

Some idea of Whitman's capacity for dramatic narration may be gained from the following lines taken from "Not a Man, and Yet a Man," a poem of even greater length than "The Rape of Florida":

> *"A flash of steely lightning from his hand,*
> *Strikes down the groaning leader of the band;*
> *Divides his startled comrades, and again*
> *Descending, leaves fair Dora's captors slain.*
> *Her, seizing then within a strong embrace,*
> *Out in the dark he wheels his flying pace;*
>
> *He speaks not, but with stalwart tenderness*
> *Her swelling bosom firm to his doth press;*
> *Springs like a stag that flees the eager hound,*
> *And like a whirlwind rustles o'er the ground.*
> *Her locks swim in dishevelled wildness o'er*
> *His shoulders, streaming to his waist and more;*
> *While on and on, strong as a rolling flood,*
> *His sweeping footsteps part the silent wood."*

It is curious and interesting to trace the growth of individuality and race consciousness in this group of poets. Jupiter Hammon's verses were almost entirely religious exhortations. Only very seldom does Phillis Wheatley sound a native note. Four times in single lines she refers to herself as "Afric's muse." In a poem of admonition addressed to the students at the "University of Cambridge in New England" she refers to herself as follows:

> *"Ye blooming plants of human race divine,*
> *An Ethiop tells you 'tis your greatest foe."*

But one looks in vain for some outburst or even complaint against the bondage of her people, for some agonizing cry about her native land. In two poems she refers definitely to Africa as her home, but in each instance there seems to be under the sentiment of the lines a feeling of almost smug contentment at her own escape therefrom. In the poem, "On Being Brought from Africa to America," she says:

> *"'Twas mercy brought me from my pagan land,*
> *Taught my benighted soul to understand*
> *That there's a God and there's a Saviour too;*
> *Once I redemption neither sought or knew.*
> *Some view our sable race with scornful eye,*
> *'Their color is a diabolic dye.'*

> Remember, Christians, Negroes black as Cain,
> May be refined, and join th' angelic train."

In the poem addressed to the Earl of Dartmouth, she speaks of freedom and makes a reference to the parents from whom she was taken as a child, a reference which cannot but strike the reader as rather unimpassioned:

> "Should you, my lord, while you peruse my song,
> Wonder from whence my love of Freedom sprung,
> Whence flow these wishes for the common good,
> By feeling hearts alone best understood;
> I, young in life, by seeming cruel fate
> Was snatch'd from Afric's fancy'd happy seat;
> What pangs excruciating must molest,
> What sorrows labor in my parents' breast?
> Steel'd was that soul and by no misery mov'd
> That from a father seiz'd his babe belov'd;
> Such, such my case. And can I then but pray
> Others may never feel tyrannic sway?"

The bulk of Phillis Wheatley's work consists of poems addressed to people of prominence. Her book was dedicated to the Countess of Huntington, at whose house she spent the greater part of her time while in England. On his repeal of the Stamp Act, she wrote a poem to King George III, whom she saw later; another poem she wrote to the Earl of Dartmouth, whom she knew. A number of her verses were addressed to other persons of distinction. Indeed, it is apparent that Phillis was far from being a democrat. She was far from being a democrat not only in her social ideas but also in her political ideas; unless a religious meaning is given to the closing lines of her ode to General Washington, she was a decided royalist:

> "A crown, a mansion, and a throne that shine
> With gold unfading, Washington! be thine."

Nevertheless, she was an ardent patriot. Her ode to General Washington (1775), her spirited poem, "On Major General Lee" (1776) and her poem, "Liberty and Peace," written in celebration of the close of the war, reveal not only strong patriotic feeling but an understanding of the issues at stake. In her poem, "On Major General Lee," she makes her hero reply thus to the taunts of the British commander into whose hands he has been delivered through treachery:

"O arrogance of tongue!
And wild ambition, ever prone to wrong!
Believ'st thou, chief, that armies such as thine
Can stretch in dust that heaven-defended line?
In vain allies may swarm from distant lands,
And demons aid in formidable bands,
Great as thou art, thou shun'st the field of fame,
Disgrace to Britain and the British name!
When offer'd combat by the noble foe,
(Foe to misrule) why did the sword forego
The easy conquest of the rebel-land?
Perhaps Too easy for thy martial hand.

What various causes to the field invite!
For plunder YOU, and we for freedom fight,
Her cause divine with generous ardor fires,
And every bosom glows as she inspires!
Already thousands of your troops have fled
To the drear mansions of the silent dead:
Columbia, too, beholds with streaming eyes
Her heroes fall—'tis freedom's sacrifice!
So wills the power who with convulsive storms
Shakes impious realms, and nature's face deforms;
Yet those brave troops, innum'rous as the sands,
One soul inspires, one General Chief commands;
Find in your train of boasted heroes, one
To match the praise of Godlike Washington.
Thrice happy Chief in whom the virtues join,
And heaven taught prudence speaks the man divine."

What Phillis Wheatley failed to achieve is due in no small degree to her education and environment. Her mind was steeped in the classics; her verses are filled with classical and mythological allusions. She knew Ovid thoroughly and was familiar with other

Latin authors. She must have known Alexander Pope by heart. And, too, she was reared and sheltered in a wealthy and cultured family,—a wealthy and cultured Boston family; she never had the opportunity to learn life; she never found out her own true relation to life and to her surroundings. And it should not be forgotten that she was only about thirty years old when she died. The impulse or the compulsion that might have driven her genius off the worn paths, out on a journey of exploration, Phillis Wheatley never received. But, whatever her limitations, she merits more than America has accorded her.

Horton, who was born three years after Phillis Wheatley's death, expressed in all of his poetry strong complaint at his condition of slavery and a deep longing for freedom. The following verses are typical of his style and his ability:

> *"Alas! and am I born for this,*
> *To wear this slavish chain?*
> *Deprived of all created bliss,*
> *Through hardship, toil, and pain?*
>
> *   *   *   *   *
>
> *Come, Liberty! thou cheerful sound,*
> *Roll through my ravished ears;*
> *Come, let my grief in joys be drowned,*
> *And drive away my fears."*

In Mrs. Harper we find something more than the complaint and the longing of Horton. We find an expression of a sense of wrong and injustice. The following stanzas are from a poem addressed to the white women of America:

> *"You can sigh o'er the sad-eyed Armenian*
> *Who weeps in her desolate home.*
> *You can mourn o'er the exile of Russia*
> *From kindred and friends doomed to roam.*
>
> *   *   *   *   *
>
> *But hark! from our Southland are floating*
> *Sobs of anguish, murmurs of pain,*

And women heart-stricken are weeping
O'er their tortured and slain.

* * * * *

Have ye not, oh, my favored sisters,
Just a plea, a prayer or a tear
For mothers who dwell 'neath the shadows
Of agony, hatred and fear?

* * * * *

Weep not, oh my well sheltered sisters,
Weep not for the Negro alone,
But weep for your sons who must gather
The crops which their fathers have sown."

Whitman, in the midst of "The Rape of Florida," a poem in which he related the taking of the State of Florida from the Seminoles, stops and discusses the race question. He discusses it in many other poems; and he discusses it from many different angles. In Whitman we find not only an expression of a sense of wrong and injustice, but we hear a note of faith and a note also of defiance. For example, in the opening to Canto II of "The Rape of Florida":

"Greatness by nature cannot be entailed;
It is an office ending with the man,—
Sage, hero, Saviour, tho' the Sire be hailed,
The son may reach obscurity in the van:
Sublime achievements know no patent plan,
Man's immortality's a book with seals,
And none but God shall open—none else can—
But opened, it the mystery reveals,—
Manhood's conquest of man to heaven's respect appeals.

"Is manhood less because man's face is black?
Let thunders of the loosened seals reply!
Who shall the rider's restive steed turn back,
Or who withstand the arrows he lets fly
Between the mountains of eternity?
Genius ride forth! Thou gift and torch of heav'n!

JAMES WELDON JOHNSON

The mastery is kindled in thine eye;
To conquest ride! thy bow of strength is giv'n—
The trampled hordes of caste before thee shall be driv'n!

*   *   *   *   *

"'Tis hard to judge if hatred of one's race,
By those who deem themselves superior-born,
Be worse than that quiescence in disgrace,
Which only merits—and should only—scorn.
Oh, let me see the Negro night and morn,
Pressing and fighting in, for place and power!
All earth is place—all time th' auspicious hour,
While heaven leans forth to look, oh, will he quail or cower?

"Ah! I abhor his protest and complaint!
His pious looks and patience I despise!
He can't evade the test, disguised as saint;
The manly voice of freedom bids him rise,
And shake himself before Philistine eyes!
And, like a lion roused, no sooner than
A foe dare come, play all his energies,
And court the fray with fury if he can;
For hell itself respects a fearless, manly man."

It may be said that none of these poets strike a deep native strain or sound a distinctively original note, either in matter or form. That is true; but the same thing may be said of all the American poets down to the writers of the present generation, with the exception of Poe and Walt Whitman. The thing in which these black poets are mostly excelled by their contemporaries is mere technique.

Paul Laurence Dunbar stands out as the first poet from the Negro race in the United States to show a combined mastery over poetic material and poetic technique, to reveal innate literary distinction in what he wrote, and to maintain a high level of performance. He was the first to rise to a height from which he could take a perspective view of his own race. He was the first to see objectively its humor, its superstitions, its shortcomings; the first to feel sympathetically its heart-wounds, its yearnings, its aspirations, and to voice them all in a purely literary form.

Dunbar's fame rests chiefly on his poems in Negro dialect. This appraisal of him is, no doubt, fair; for in these dialect poems he not only carried his art to the highest point of perfection, but he made a contribution to American literature unlike what any one else had made, a contribution which, perhaps, no one else could have made. Of course, Negro dialect poetry was written before Dunbar wrote, most of it by white writers; but the fact stands out that Dunbar was the first to use it as a medium for the true interpretation of Negro character and psychology. And, yet, dialect poetry does not constitute the whole or even the bulk of Dunbar's work. In addition to a large number of poems of a very high order done in literary English, he was the author of four novels and several volumes of short stories.

Indeed, Dunbar did not begin his career as a writer of dialect. I may be pardoned for introducing here a bit of reminiscence. My personal friendship with Paul Dunbar began before he had achieved recognition, and continued to be close until his death. When I first met him he had published a thin volume, "Oak and Ivy," which was being sold chiefly through his own efforts. "Oak and Ivy" showed no distinctive Negro influence, but rather the influence of James Whitcomb Riley. At this time Paul and I were together every day for several months. He talked to me a great deal about his hopes and ambitions. In these talks he revealed that he had reached a realization of the possibilities of poetry in the dialect, together with a recognition of the fact that it offered the surest way by which he could get a hearing. Often he said to me: "I've got to write dialect poetry; it's the only way I can get them to listen to me." I was with Dunbar at the beginning of what proved to be his last illness. He said to me then: "I have not grown. I am writing the same things I wrote ten years ago, and am writing them no better." His self-accusation was not fully true; he had grown, and he had gained a surer control of his art, but he had not accomplished the greater things of which he was constantly dreaming; the public had held him to the things for which it had accorded him recognition. If Dunbar had lived he would have achieved some of those dreams, but even while he talked so dejectedly to me he seemed to feel that he was not to live. He died when he was only thirty-three.

It has a bearing on this entire subject to note that Dunbar was of unmixed Negro blood; so, as the greatest figure in literature which the colored race in the United States has produced, he stands as an example at once refuting and confounding those who wish to believe that whatever extraordinary ability an Aframerican shows is due to an admixture of white blood.

As a man, Dunbar was kind and tender. In conversation he was brilliant and polished. His voice was his chief charm, and was a great element in his success as a reader of his own works. In his actions he was impulsive as a child, sometimes even erratic; indeed, his intimate friends almost looked upon him as a spoiled boy. He was always delicate in health. Temperamentally, he belonged to that class of poets who Taine says are vessels too weak to contain the spirit of poetry, the poets whom poetry kills, the Byrons, the Burns's, the De Mussets, the Poes.

To whom may he be compared, this boy who scribbled his early verses while he ran an elevator, whose youth was a battle against poverty, and who, in spite of almost insurmountable obstacles, rose to success? A comparison between him and Burns is not unfitting. The similarity between many phases of their lives is remarkable, and their works are not incommensurable. Burns took the strong dialect of his people and made it classic; Dunbar took the humble speech of his people and in it wrought music.

Mention of Dunbar brings up for consideration the fact that, although he is the most outstanding figure in literature among the Aframericans of the United States, he does not stand alone among the Aframericans of the whole Western world. There are Plácido and Manzano in Cuba; Vieux and Durand in Haiti, Machado de Assis in Brazil; Leon Laviaux in Martinique, and others still that might be mentioned, who stand on a plane with or even above Dunbar. Plácido and Machado de Assis rank as great in the literatures of their respective countries without any qualifications whatever. They are world figures in the literature of the Latin languages. Machado de Assis is somewhat handicapped in this respect by having as his tongue and medium the lesser known Portuguese, but Plácido, writing in the language of Spain, Mexico, Cuba and of almost the whole of South America, is universally known. His works have been republished in the original in Spain, Mexico and in most of the Latin-American countries; several editions have been published in the United States; translations of his works have been made into French and German.

Plácido is in some respects the greatest of all the Cuban poets. In sheer genius and the fire of inspiration he surpasses even the more finished Heredia. Then, too, his birth, his life and his death ideally contained the tragic elements that go into the making of a halo about a poet's head. Plácido was born in Habana in 1809. The first months of his life were passed in a foundling asylum; indeed, his real name, Gabriel de la Concepcion Valdés, was in honor of its founder. His father took him out of the asylum, but shortly afterwards went to Mexico and died there. His early life was a struggle against poverty; his youth and manhood was a struggle for Cuban independence. His death placed him in the list of Cuban martyrs. On the 27th of June, 1844, he was lined up against a wall with ten others and shot by order of the Spanish authorities on a charge of conspiracy. In his short but eventful life he turned out work which bulks more than six hundred pages. During the few hours preceding his execution he wrote three of his best known poems, among them his famous sonnet, "Mother, Farewell!"

Plácido's sonnet to his mother has been translated into every important language; William Cullen Bryant did it in English; but in spite of its wide popularity, it is, perhaps, outside of Cuba the least understood of all Plácido's poems. It is curious to note how Bryant's translation totally misses the intimate sense of the delicate subtility of the poem. The American poet makes it a tender and loving farewell of a son who is about to die to a heart-broken mother; but that is not the kind of a farewell that Plácido intended to write or did write.

The key to the poem is in the first word, and the first word is the Spanish conjunction *Si* (if). The central idea, then, of the sonnet is, "If the sad fate which now overwhelms me should bring a pang to your heart, do not weep, for I die a glorious death and sound the last note of my lyre to you." Bryant either failed to understand or ignored the opening word, "If," because he was not familiar with the poet's history.

While Plácido's father was a Negro, his mother was a Spanish white woman, a dancer in one of the Habana theatres. At his birth she abandoned him to a foundling asylum, and perhaps never saw him again, although it is known that she outlived her son. When the poet came down to his last hours he remembered that somewhere there lived a woman who was his mother; that although she had heartlessly abandoned him; that although he owed her no filial duty, still she might, perhaps, on hearing of his sad end feel some pang of grief or sadness; so he tells her in his last words that he dies happy and bids her not to weep. This he does with nobility and dignity, but absolutely without affection. Taking into account these facts, and especially their humiliating and embittering effect upon a soul so sensitive as Plácido's, this sonnet, in spite of the obvious weakness of the sestet as compared with the octave, is a remarkable piece of work.[1]

In considering the Aframerican poets of the Latin languages I am impelled to think that, as up to this time the colored poets of greater universality have come out of the Latin-American countries rather than out of the United States, they will continue to do so for a good many years. The reason for this I hinted at in the first part of this preface. The colored poet in the United States labors within limitations which he cannot easily pass over. He is always on the defensive or the offensive. The pressure upon him to be propagandic is well nigh irresistible. These conditions are suffocating to breadth and to real art in poetry. In addition he labors under the handicap of finding culture not entirely colorless in the United States. On the other hand, the colored poet of Latin-America can voice the national spirit without any reservations. And he will be rewarded without any reservations, whether it be to place him among the great or declare him the greatest.

So I think it probable that the first world-acknowledged Aframerican poet will come out of Latin-America. Over against this probability, of course, is the great advantage possessed by the colored poet in the United States of writing in the world-conquering English language.

This preface has gone far beyond what I had in mind when I started. It was my intention to gather together the best verses I could find by Negro poets and present them with a bare word of introduction. It was not my plan to make this collection inclusive nor to make the book in any sense a book of criticism. I planned to present only verses by contemporary writers; but, perhaps, because this is the first collection of its kind, I realized the absence of a starting-point and was led to provide one and to fill in with historical data what I felt to be a gap.

It may be surprising to many to see how little of the poetry being written by Negro poets to-day is being written in Negro dialect. The newer Negro poets show a tendency to discard dialect; much of the subject-matter which went into the making of traditional dialect poetry, 'possums, watermelons, etc., they have discarded altogether, at least, as poetic material. This tendency will, no doubt, be regretted by the majority of white readers; and, indeed, it would be a distinct loss if the American Negro poets threw away this quaint and musical folk-speech as a medium of expression. And yet, after all, these

---

1. Plácido's sonnet and two English versions will be found in the Appendix.

poets are working through a problem not realized by the reader, and, perhaps, by many of these poets themselves not realized consciously. They are trying to break away from, not Negro dialect itself, but the limitations on Negro dialect imposed by the fixing effects of long convention.

The Negro in the United States has achieved or been placed in a certain artistic niche. When he is thought of artistically, it is as a happy-go-lucky, singing, shuffling, banjo-picking being or as a more or less pathetic figure. The picture of him is in a log cabin amid fields of cotton or along the levees. Negro dialect is naturally and by long association the exact instrument for voicing this phase of Negro life; and by that very exactness it is an instrument with but two full stops, humor and pathos. So even when he confines himself to purely racial themes, the Aframerican poet realizes that there are phases of Negro life in the United States which cannot be treated in the dialect either adequately or artistically. Take, for example, the phases rising out of life in Harlem, that most wonderful Negro city in the world. I do not deny that a Negro in a log cabin is more picturesque than a Negro in a Harlem flat, but the Negro in the Harlem flat is here, and he is but part of a group growing everywhere in the country, a group whose ideals are becoming increasingly more vital than those of the traditionally artistic group, even if its members are less picturesque.

What the colored poet in the United States needs to do is something like what Synge did for the Irish; he needs to find a form that will express the racial spirit by symbols from within rather than by symbols from without, such as the mere mutilation of English spelling and pronunciation. He needs a form that is freer and larger than dialect, but which will still hold the racial flavor; a form expressing the imagery, the idioms, the peculiar turns of thought, and the distinctive humor and pathos, too, of the Negro, but which will also be capable of voicing the deepest and highest emotions and aspirations, and allow of the widest range of subjects and the widest scope of treatment.

Negro dialect is at present a medium that is not capable of giving expression to the varied conditions of Negro life in America, and much less is it capable of giving the fullest interpretation of Negro character and psychology. This is no indictment against the dialect as dialect, but against the mould of convention in which Negro dialect in the United States has been set. In time these conventions may become lost, and the colored poet in the United States may sit down to write in dialect

JAMES WELDON JOHNSON

without feeling that his first line will put the general reader in a frame of mind which demands that the poem be humorous or pathetic. In the meantime, there is no reason why these poets should not continue to do the beautiful things that can be done, and done best, in the dialect.

In stating the need for Aframerican poets in the United States to work out a new and distinctive form of expression I do not wish to be understood to hold any theory that they should limit themselves to Negro poetry, to racial themes; the sooner they are able to write *American* poetry spontaneously, the better. Nevertheless, I believe that the richest contribution the Negro poet can make to the American literature of the future will be the fusion into it of his own individual artistic gifts.

Not many of the writers here included, except Dunbar, are known at all to the general reading public; and there is only one of these who has a widely recognized position in the American literary world, he is William Stanley Braithwaite. Mr. Braithwaite is not only unique in this respect, but he stands unique among all the Aframerican writers the United States has yet produced. He has gained his place, taking as the standard and measure for his work the identical standard and measure applied to American writers and American literature. He has asked for no allowances or rewards, either directly or indirectly, on account of his race.

Mr. Braithwaite is the author of two volumes of verses, lyrics of delicate and tenuous beauty. In his more recent and uncollected poems he shows himself more and more decidedly the mystic. But his place in American literature is due more to his work as a critic and anthologist than to his work as a poet. There is still another role he has played, that of friend of poetry and poets. It is a recognized fact that in the work which preceded the present revival of poetry in the United States, no one rendered more unremitting and valuable service than Mr. Braithwaite. And it can be said that no future study of American poetry of this age can be made without reference to Braithwaite.

Two authors included in the book are better known for their work in prose than in poetry: W.E.B. Du Bois whose well-known prose at its best is, however, impassioned and rhythmical; and Benjamin Brawley who is the author, among other works, of one of the best handbooks on the English drama that has yet appeared in America.

But the group of the new Negro poets, whose work makes up the bulk of this anthology, contains names destined to be known. Claude

McKay, although still quite a young man, has already demonstrated his power, breadth and skill as a poet. Mr. McKay's breadth is as essential a part of his equipment as his power and skill. He demonstrates mastery of the three when as a Negro poet he pours out the bitterness and rebellion in his heart in those two sonnet-tragedies, "If We Must Die" and "To the White Fiends," in a manner that strikes terror; and when as a cosmic poet he creates the atmosphere and mood of poetic beauty in the absolute, as he does in "Spring in New Hampshire" and "The Harlem Dancer." Mr. McKay gives evidence that he has passed beyond the danger which threatens many of the new Negro poets—the danger of allowing the purely polemical phases of the race problem to choke their sense of artistry.

Mr. McKay's earliest work is unknown in this country. It consists of poems written and published in his native Jamaica. I was fortunate enough to run across this first volume, and I could not refrain from reproducing here one of the poems written in the West Indian Negro dialect. I have done this not only to illustrate the widest range of the poet's talent and to offer a comparison between the American and the West Indian dialects, but on account of the intrinsic worth of the poem itself. I was much tempted to introduce several more, in spite of the fact that they might require a glossary, because however greater work Mr. McKay may do he can never do anything more touching and charming than these poems in the Jamaica dialect.

Fenton Johnson is a young poet of the ultra-modern school who gives promise of greater work than he has yet done. Jessie Fauset shows that she possesses the lyric gift, and she works with care and finish. Miss Fauset is especially adept in her translations from the French. Georgia Douglas Johnson is a poet neither afraid nor ashamed of her emotions. She limits herself to the purely conventional forms, rhythms and rhymes, but through them she achieves striking effects. The principal theme of Mrs. Johnson's poems is the secret dread down in every woman's heart, the dread of the passing of youth and beauty, and with them love. An old theme, one which poets themselves have often wearied of, but which, like death, remains one of the imperishable themes on which is made the poetry that has moved men's hearts through all ages. In her ingenuously wrought verses, through sheer simplicity and spontaneousness, Mrs. Johnson often sounds a note of pathos or passion that will not fail to waken a response, except in those too sophisticated or cynical to respond to natural impulses. Of the half dozen or so of colored women writing creditable verse, Anne Spencer is the most modern and least obvious in her methods. Her lines are at times involved and turgid and almost cryptic, but she shows an originality which does not depend upon eccentricities. In her "Before the Feast of Shushan" she displays an opulence, the love of which has long been charged against the Negro as one of his naïve and childish traits, but which in art may infuse a much needed color, warmth and spirit of abandon into American poetry.

John W. Holloway, more than any Negro poet writing in the dialect to-day, summons to his work the lilt, the spontaneity and charm of which Dunbar was the supreme master whenever he employed that medium. It is well to say a word here about the dialect poems of James Edwin Campbell. In dialect, Campbell was a precursor of Dunbar. A comparison of his idioms and phonetics with those of Dunbar reveals great differences. Dunbar is a shade or two more sophisticated and his phonetics approach nearer to a mean standard of the dialects spoken in the different sections. Campbell is more primitive and his phonetics are those of the dialect as spoken by the Negroes of the sea islands off the coasts of South Carolina and Georgia, which to this day remains comparatively close to its African roots, and is strikingly similar to the speech of the uneducated Negroes of the West Indies. An error that confuses many persons in reading or understanding Negro dialect is the idea that it is uniform. An ignorant Negro of the uplands of Georgia would have almost as much difficulty in understanding an ignorant sea island Negro as an Englishman would have. Not even in the dialect of any particular section is a given word always pronounced in precisely the same way. Its pronunciation depends upon the preceding and following sounds. Sometimes the combination permits of a liaison so close that to the uninitiated the sound of the word is almost completely lost.

The constant effort in Negro dialect is to elide all troublesome consonants and sounds. This negative effort may be after all only positive laziness of the vocal organs, but the result is a softening and smoothing which makes Negro dialect so delightfully easy for singers.

Daniel Webster Davis wrote dialect poetry at the time when Dunbar was writing. He gained great popularity, but it did not spread beyond his own race. Davis had unctuous humor, but he was crude. For illustration, note the vast stretch between his "Hog Meat" and Dunbar's "When de Co'n Pone's Hot," both of them poems on the traditional ecstasy of the Negro in contemplation of "good things" to eat.

It is regrettable that two of the most gifted writers included were cut off so early in life. R. C. Jamison and Joseph S. Cotter, Jr., died several years ago, both of them in their youth. Jamison was barely thirty at the time of his death, but among his poems there is one, at least, which stamps him as a poet of superior talent and lofty inspiration. "The Negro Soldiers" is a poem with the race problem as its theme, yet it transcends the limits of race and rises to a spiritual height that makes it one of the noblest poems of the Great War. Cotter died a mere boy of twenty, and the latter part of that brief period he passed in an invalid state. Some months before his death he published a thin volume of verses which were for the most part written on a sick bed. In this little volume Cotter showed fine poetic sense and a free and bold mastery over his material. A reading of Cotter's poems is certain to induce that mood in which one will regretfully speculate on what the young poet might have accomplished had he not been cut off so soon.

As intimated above, my original idea for this book underwent a change in the writing of the introduction. I first planned to select twenty-five to thirty poems which I judged to be up to a certain standard, and offer them with a few words of introduction and without comment. In the collection, as it grew to be, that "certain standard" has been broadened if not lowered; but I believe that this is offset by the advantage of the wider range given the reader and the student of the subject.

I offer this collection without making apology or asking allowance. I feel confident that the reader will find not only an earnest for the future, but actual achievement. The reader cannot but be impressed by the distance already covered. It is a long way from the plaints of George Horton to the invectives of Claude McKay, from the obviousness of Frances Harper to the complexness of Anne Spencer. Much ground has been covered, but more will yet be covered. It is this side of prophecy to declare that the undeniable creative genius of the Negro is destined to make a distinctive and valuable contribution to American poetry.

I wish to extend my thanks to Mr. Arthur A. Schomburg, who placed his valuable collection of books by Negro authors at my disposal. I wish also to acknowledge with thanks the kindness of Dodd, Mead & Co. for permitting the reprint of poems by Paul Laurence Dunbar; of the Cornhill Publishing Company for permission to reprint poems of Georgia Douglas Johnson, Joseph S. Cotter, Jr., Bertram Johnson and Waverley Carmichael; and of Neale & Co. for permission to reprint poems of John W. Holloway. I wish to thank Mr. Braithwaite for permission to use the included poems from his forthcoming volume, "Sandy Star and Willie Gee." And to acknowledge the courtesy of the following magazines: *The Crisis, The Century Magazine, The Liberator, The Freeman, The Independent, Others*, and *Poetry: A Magazine of Verse*.

James Weldon Johnson.
New York City, 1921.

PAUL LAURENCE DUNBAR

A Negro Love Song[1]

Seen my lady home las' night,
    Jump back, honey, jump back.
Hel' huh han' an' sque'z it tight,
    Jump back, honey, jump back.
Hyeahd huh sigh a little sigh,
Seen a light gleam f'om huh eye,
An' a smile go flittin' by—
    Jump back, honey, jump back.

Hyeahd de win' blow thoo de pine,
    Jump back, honey, jump back.
Mockin'-bird was singin' fine,
    Jump back, honey, jump back.
An' my hea't was beatin' so,
When I reached my lady's do',
Dat I could n't ba' to go—
    Jump back, honey, jump back.

Put my ahm aroun' huh wais',
    Jump back, honey, jump back.
Raised huh lips an' took a tase,
    Jump back, honey, jump back.
Love me, honey, love me true?
Love me well ez I love you?
An' she answe'd, "Cose I do"—
    Jump back, honey, jump back.

---

1. Copyright by Dodd, Mead & Company.

PAUL LAURENCE DUNBAR

LITTLE BROWN BABY

Little brown baby wif spa'klin' eyes,
    Come to yo' pappy an' set on his knee.
What you been doin', suh—makin' san' pies?
    Look at dat bib—You's ez du'ty ez me.
Look at dat mouf—dat's merlasses, I bet;
    Come hyeah, Maria, an' wipe off his han's.
Bees gwine to ketch you an' eat you up yit,
    Bein' so sticky an' sweet—goodness lan's!

Little brown baby wif spa'klin' eyes
    Who's pappy's darlin' an' who's pappy's chile?
Who is it all de day nevah once tries
    Fu' to be cross, er once loses dat smile?
Whah did you git dem teef? My, you's a scamp!
    Whah did dat dimple come f'om in yo' chin?
Pappy do' know you—I b'lieves you's a tramp;
    Mammy, dis hyeah's some ol' straggler got in!

Let's th'ow him outen de do' in de san',
We do' want stragglers a-layin' 'roun' hyeah;
Let's gin him 'way to de big buggah-man;
    I know he's hidin' erroun' hyeah right neah.
Buggah-man, buggah-man, come in de do',
    Hyeah's a bad boy you kin have fu' to eat.
Mammy an' pappy do' want him no mo',
    Swaller him down f'om his haid to his feet!

Dah, now, I t'ought dat you'd hug me up close.
    Go back, ol' buggah, you sha'n't have dis boy.
He ain't no tramp, ner no straggler, of co'se;
    He's pappy's pa'dner an' playmate an' joy.
Come to you' pallet now—go to you' res';
    Wisht you could allus know ease an' cleah skies;
Wisht you could stay jes' a chile on my breas'—
    Little brown baby wif spa'klin' eyes!

PAUL LAURENCE DUNBAR

Ships That Pass in the Night

Out in the sky the great dark clouds are massing;
    I look far out into the pregnant night,
Where I can hear a solemn booming gun
    And catch the gleaming of a random light,
That tells me that the ship I seek is passing, passing.

My tearful eyes my soul's deep hurt are glassing;
    For I would hail and check that ship of ships.
I stretch my hands imploring, cry aloud,
    My voice falls dead a foot from mine own lips,
And but its ghost doth reach that vessel, passing, passing.

O Earth, O Sky, O Ocean, both surpassing,
    O heart of mine, O soul that dreads the dark!
Is there no hope for me? Is there no way
    That I may sight and check that speeding bark
Which out of sight and sound is passing, passing?

Lover's Lane

Summah night an' sighin' breeze,
    'Long de lovah's lane;
Frien'ly, shadder-mekin' trees,
    'Long de lovah's lane.
White folks' wo'k all done up gran'—
Me an' 'Mandy han'-in-han'
Struttin' lak we owned de lan',
    'Long de lovah's lane.

Owl a-settin' 'side de road,
    'Long de lovah's lane,
Lookin' at us lak he knowed
    Dis uz lovah's lane.
Go on, hoot yo' Mou'nful tune,
You ain' nevah loved in June,
An' come hidin' f'om de moon
    Down in lovah's lane.

Bush it ben' an' nod an' sway,
    Down in lovah's lane,
Try'n' to hyeah me whut I say
    'Long de lovah's lane.
But I whispahs low lak dis,
An' my 'Mandy smile huh bliss—
Mistah Bush he shek his fis',
    Down in lovah's lane.

Whut I keer ef day is long,
    Down in lovah's lane.
I kin allus sing a song
    'Long de lovah's lane.
An' de wo'ds I hyeah an' say
Meks up fu' de weary day
Wen I's strollin' by de way,
    Down in lovah's lane.

An' dis t'ought will allus rise
    Down in lovah's lane;
Wondah whethah in de skies
    Dey's a lovah's lane.
Ef dey ain't, I tell you true,
'Ligion do look mighty blue,
'Cause I do' know whut I'd do
    'Dout a lovah's lane.

The Debt

This is the debt I pay
Just for one riotous day,
Years of regret and grief.
Sorrow without relief.

Pay it I will to the end—
Until the grave, my friend,
Gives me a true release—
Gives me the clasp of peace.

Slight was the thing I bought,
Small was the debt I thought,
Poor was the loan at best—
God! but the interest!

The Haunted Oak

Pray why are you so bare, so bare,
    Oh, bough of the old oak-tree;
And why, when I go through the shade you throw,
    Runs a shudder over me?

My leaves were green as the best, I trow,
    And sap ran free in my veins,
But I saw in the moonlight dim and weird
    A guiltless victim's pains.

I bent me down to hear his sigh;
    I shook with his gurgling moan,
And I trembled sore when they rode away,
    And left him here alone.

They'd charged him with the old, old crime,
    And set him fast in jail:
Oh, why does the dog howl all night long,
    And why does the night wind wail?

He prayed his prayer and he swore his oath,
    And he raised his hand to the sky;
But the beat of hoofs smote on his ear,
    And the steady tread drew nigh.

Who is it rides by night, by night,
    Over the moonlit road?
And what is the spur that keeps the pace,
    What is the galling goad?

And now they beat at the prison door,
    "Ho, keeper, do not stay!
We are friends of him whom you hold within,
    And we fain would take him away

From those who ride fast on our heels
 With mind to do him wrong;
They have no care for his innocence,
 And the rope they bear is long."

They have fooled the jailer with lying words,
 They have fooled the man with lies;
The bolts unbar, the locks are drawn,
 And the great door open flies.

Now they have taken him from the jail,
 And hard and fast they ride,
And the leader laughs low down in his throat,
 As they halt my trunk beside.

Oh, the judge, he wore a mask of black,
 And the doctor one of white,
And the minister, with his oldest son,
 Was curiously bedight.

Oh, foolish man, why weep you now?
 'Tis but a little space,
And the time will come when these shall dread
 The mem'ry of your face.

I feel the rope against my bark,
 And the weight of him in my grain,
I feel in the throe of his final woe
 The touch of my own last pain.

And never more shall leaves come forth
 On a bough that bears the ban;
I am burned with dread, I am dried and dead,
 From the curse of a guiltless man.

And ever the judge rides by, rides by,
 And goes to hunt the deer,
And ever another rides his soul
 In the guise of a mortal fear.

  PAUL LAURENCE DUNBAR

And ever the man he rides me hard,
    And never a night stays he;
For I feel his curse as a haunted bough
    On the trunk of a haunted tree.

When de Co'n Pone's Hot

Dey is times in life when Nature
    Seems to slip a cog an' go,
Jes' a-rattlin' down creation,
    Lak an ocean's overflow;
When de worl' jes' stahts a-spinnin'
    Lak a picaninny's top,
An' yo' cup o' joy is brimmin'
    'Twell it seems about to slop,
An' you feel jes' lak a racah,
    Dat is trainin' fu' to trot—
When yo' mammy says de blessin'
    An' de co'n pone's hot.

When you set down at de table,
    Kin' o' weary lak an' sad,
An' you'se jes' a little tiahed
    An' purhaps a little mad;
How yo' gloom tu'ns into gladness,
    How yo' joy drives out de doubt
When de oven do' is opened,
    An' de smell comes po'in' out;
Why, de 'lectric light o' Heaven
    Seems to settle on de spot,
When yo' mammy says de blessin'
    An' de co'n pone's hot.

When de cabbage pot is steamin'
    An' de bacon good an' fat,
When de chittlins is a-sputter'n'
    So's to show you whah dey's at;
Tek away yo' sody biscuit,
    Tek away yo' cake an' pie,
Fu' de glory time is comin',
    An' it's 'proachin' mighty nigh,

           PAUL LAURENCE DUNBAR

An' you want to jump an' hollah,
　　Dough you know you'd bettah not,
When yo' mammy says de blessin'
　　An' de co'n pone's hot.

I have hyeahd o' lots o' sermons,
　　An' I've hyeahd o' lots o' prayers,
An' I've listened to some singin'
　　Dat has tuck me up de stairs
Of de Glory-Lan' an' set me
　　Jes' below de Mastah's th'one,
An' have lef my hea't a-singin'
　　In a happy aftah tone;
But dem wu'ds so sweetly murmured
　　Seem to tech de softes' spot,
When my mammy says de blessin',
　　An' de co'n pone's hot.

A Death Song

Lay me down beneaf de willers in de grass,
Whah de branch'll go a-singin' as it pass
    An' w'en I's a-layin' low,
    I kin hyeah it as it go
Singin', "Sleep, my honey, tek yo' res' at las'."

Lay me nigh to whah hit meks a little pool,
An' de watah stan's so quiet lak an' cool,
    Whah de little birds in spring,
    Ust to come an' drink an' sing,
An' de chillen waded on dey way to school.

Let me settle w'en my shouldahs draps dey load
Nigh enough to hyeah de noises in de road;
    Fu' I t'ink de las' long res'
    Gwine to soothe my sperrit bes'
If I's layin' 'mong de t'ings I's allus knowed.

JAMES EDWIN CAMPBELL

Negro Serenade

O, de light-bugs glimmer down de lane,
　　Merlindy! Merlindy!
O, de whip'-will callin' notes ur pain—
　　Merlindy, O, Merlindy!
O, honey lub, my turkle dub,
　　Doan' you hyuh my bawnjer ringin',
While de night-dew falls an' de ho'n owl calls
　　By de ol' ba'n gate Ise singin'.

O, Miss 'Lindy, doan' you hyuh me, chil',
　　Merlindy! Merlindy!
My lub fur you des dribe me wil'—
　　Merlindy, O, Merlindy!
I'll sing dis night twel broad day-light,
　　Ur bu's' my froat wid tryin',
'Less you come down, Miss 'Lindy Brown,
　　An' stops dis ha't f'um sighin'!

De Cunjah Man

O chillen, run, de Cunjah man,
Him mouf ez beeg ez fryin' pan,
Him yurs am small, him eyes am raid,
Him hab no toof een him ol' haid,
Him hab him roots, him wu'k him trick,
Him roll him eye, him mek you sick—
 De Cunjah man, de Cunjah man,
 O chillen, run, de Cunjah man!

Him hab ur ball ob raid, raid ha'r,
Him hide it un' de kitchen sta'r,
Mam Jude huh pars urlong dat way,
An' now huh hab ur snaik, de say.
Him wrop ur roun' huh buddy tight,
Huh eyes pop out, ur orful sight—
 De Cunjah man, de Cunjah man,
 O chillen, run, de Cunjah man!

Miss Jane, huh dribe him f'um huh do',
An' now huh hens woan' lay no mo';
De Jussey cow huh done fall sick,
Hit all done by de Cunjah trick.
Him put ur root un' 'Lijah's baid,
An' now de man he sho' am daid—
 De Cunjah man, de Cunjah man,
 O chillen, run, de Cunjah man!

Me see him stan' de yudder night
Right een de road een white moon-light;
Him toss him arms, him whirl him 'roun',
Him stomp him foot urpon de groun';
De snaiks come crawlin', one by one,
Me hyuh um hiss, me break an' run—
 De Cunjah man, de Cunjah man,
 O chillen, run, de Cunjah man!

          JAMES EDWIN CAMPBELL

Uncle Eph's Banjo Song

Clean de ba'n an' sweep de flo',
    Sing, my bawnjer, sing!
We's gwine ter dawnce dis eb'nin' sho',
    Ring, my bawnjer, ring!
Den hits up de road an' down de lane,
Hurry, niggah, you miss de train;
De yaller gal she dawnce so neat,
De yaller gal she look so sweet,
    Ring, my bawnjer, ring!

De moon come up, de sun go down,
    Sing, my bawnjer, sing!
De niggahs am all come f'um town,
    Ring, my bawnjer, ring!
Den hits roun' de hill an' froo de fiel'—
Lookout dar, niggah, doan' you steal!
De milyuns on dem vines am green,
De moon am bright, O you'll be seen,
    Ring, my bawnjer, ring!

Ol' Doc' Hyar

Ur ol' Hyar lib in ur house on de hill,
He hunner yurs ol' an' nebber wuz ill;
He yurs dee so long an' he eyes so beeg,
An' he laigs so spry dat he dawnce ur jeeg;
He lib so long dat he know ebbry tings
'Bout de beas'ses dat walks an' de bu'ds dat sings—
                    Dis Ol' Doc' Hyar,
                    Whar lib up dar
Een ur mighty fine house on ur mighty high hill.

He doctah fur all de beas'ses an' bu'ds—
He put on he specs an' he use beeg wu'ds,
He feel dee pu's' den he look mighty wise,
He pull out he watch an' he shet bofe eyes;
He grab up he hat an' grab up he cane,
Den—"blam!" go de do'—he gone lak de train,
                    Dis Ol' Doc' Hyar,
                    Whar lib up dar
Een ur mighty fine house on ur mighty high hill.

Mistah Ba'r fall sick—dee sont fur Doc' Hyar,
"O, Doctah, come queeck, an' see Mr. B'ar;
He mighty nigh daid des sho' ez you b'on!"
"Too much ur young peeg, too much ur green co'n,"
Ez he put on he hat, said Ol' Doc' Hyar;
"I'll tek 'long meh lawnce, an' lawnce Mistah B'ar,"
                    Said Ol' Doc' Hyar,
                    Whar lib up dar
Een ur mighty fine house on ur mighty high hill.

Mistah B'ar he groaned, Mistah B'ar he growled,
W'ile de ol' Miss B'ar an' de chillen howled;
Doctah Hyar tuk out he sha'p li'l lawnce,
An' pyu'ced Mistah B'ar twel he med him prawnce
Den grab up he hat an' grab up he cane
"Blam!" go de do' an' he gone lak de train,

JAMES EDWIN CAMPBELL

                    Dis Ol' Doc' Hyar,
                    Whar lib up dar
Een ur mighty fine house on ur mighty high hill.

But de vay naix day Mistah B'ar he daid;
Wen dee tell Doc' Hyar, he des scratch he haid:
"Ef pahsons git well ur pahsons git wu's,
 Money got ter come een de Ol' Hyar's pu's;
 Not wut folkses does, but fur wut dee know
 Does de folkses git paid"—an' Hyar larfed low,
                    Dis Ol' Doc' Hyar,
                    Whar lib up dar
Een de mighty fine house on de mighty high hill!

WHEN OL' SIS' JUDY PRAY

When ol' Sis' Judy pray,
De teahs come stealin' down my cheek,
De voice ur God widin me speak';
I see myse'f so po' an' weak,
Down on my knees de cross I seek,
When ol' Sis' Judy pray.

When ol' Sis' Judy pray,
De thun'ers ur Mount Sin-a-i
Comes rushin' down f'um up on high—
De Debbil tu'n his back an' fly
While sinnahs loud fur pa'don cry,
When ol' Sis' Judy pray.

When ol' Sis' Judy pray,
Ha'd sinnahs trimble in dey seat
Ter hyuh huh voice in sorro 'peat;
(While all de chu'ch des sob an' weep)
"O Shepa'd, dese, dy po' los' sheep!"
When ol' Sis' Judy pray.

When ol' Sis' Judy pray,
De whole house hit des rock an' moan
Ter see huh teahs an' hyuh huh groan;
Dar's somepin' in Sis' Judy's tone
Dat melt all ha'ts dough med ur stone
When ol' Sis' Judy pray.

When ol' Sis' Judy pray,
Salvation's light comes pourin' down—
Hit fill de chu'ch an' all de town—
Why, angels' robes go rustlin' 'roun',
An' hebben on de Yurf am foun',
When ol' Sis' Judy pray.

JAMES EDWIN CAMPBELL

When ol' Sis' Judy pray,
My soul go sweepin' up on wings,
An' loud de chu'ch wid "Glory!" rings,
An' wide de gates ur Jahsper swings
Twel you hyuh ha'ps wid golding strings,
When ol' Sis' Judy pray.

Compensation

O, rich young lord, thou ridest by
With looks of high disdain;
It chafes me not thy title high,
Thy blood of oldest strain.
The lady riding at thy side
Is but in name thy promised bride,
　　Ride on, young lord, ride on!

Her father wills and she obeys,
The custom of her class;
'Tis Land not Love the trothing sways—
For Land he sells his lass.
Her fair white hand, young lord, is thine,
Her *soul*, proud fool, her *soul* is mine,
　　Ride on, young lord, ride on!

No title high my father bore;
The tenant of thy farm,
He left me what I value more:
Clean heart, clear brain, strong arm
And love for bird and beast and bee
And song of lark and hymn of sea,
　　Ride on, young lord, ride on!

The boundless sky to me belongs,
The paltry acres thine;
The painted beauty sings thy songs,
The lavrock lilts me mine;
The hot-housed orchid blooms for thee,
The gorse and heather bloom for me,
　　Ride on, young lord, ride on!

JAMES EDWIN CAMPBELL

JAMES D. CORROTHERS

At the Closed Gate of Justice

To be a Negro in a day like this
    Demands forgiveness. Bruised with blow on blow,
Betrayed, like him whose woe dimmed eyes gave bliss
    Still must one succor those who brought one low,
To be a Negro in a day like this.

To be a Negro in a day like this
    Demands rare patience—patience that can wait
In utter darkness. 'Tis the path to miss,
    And knock, unheeded, at an iron gate,
To be a Negro in a day like this.

To be a Negro in a day like this
    Demands strange loyalty. We serve a flag
Which is to us white freedom's emphasis.
    Ah! one must love when Truth and Justice lag,
To be a Negro in a day like this.

To be a Negro in a day like this—
    Alas! Lord God, what evil have we done?
Still shines the gate, all gold and amethyst,
    But I pass by, the glorious goal unwon,
"Merely a Negro"—in a day like this!

Paul Laurence Dunbar

He came, a youth, singing in the dawn
    Of a new freedom, glowing o'er his lyre,
    Refining, as with great Apollo's fire,
    His people's gift of song. And thereupon,
This Negro singer, come to Helicon
    Constrained the masters, listening to admire,
    And roused a race to wonder and aspire,
    Gazing which way their honest voice was gone,
With ebon face uplit of glory's crest.
    Men marveled at the singer, strong and sweet,
    Who brought the cabin's mirth, the tuneful night,
But faced the morning, beautiful with light,
    To die while shadows yet fell toward the west,
    And leave his laurels at his people's feet.

Dunbar, no poet wears your laurels now;
    None rises, singing, from your race like you.
    Dark melodist, immortal, though the dew
    Fell early on the bays upon your brow,
And tinged with pathos every halcyon vow
    And brave endeavor. Silence o'er you threw
    Flowerets of love. Or, if an envious few
    Of your own people brought no garlands, how
Could Malice smite him whom the gods had crowned?
    If, like the meadow-lark, your flight was low
    Your flooded lyrics half the hilltops drowned;
A wide world heard you, and it loved you so
    It stilled its heart to list the strains you sang,
    And o'er your happy songs its plaudits rang.

JAMES D. CORROTHERS

The Negro Singer

O'er all my song the image of a face
 Lieth, like shadow on the wild sweet flowers.
 The dream, the ecstasy that prompts my powers;
 The golden lyre's delights bring little grace
To bless the singer of a lowly race.
 Long hath this mocked me: aye in marvelous hours,
 When Hera's gardens gleamed, or Cynthia's bowers,
 Or Hope's red pylons, in their far, hushed place!
But I shall dig me deeper to the gold;
 Fetch water, dripping, over desert miles,
 From clear Nyanzas and mysterious Niles
Of love; and sing, nor one kind act withhold.
 So shall men know me, and remember long,
 Nor my dark face dishonor any song.

The Road to the Bow

Ever and ever anon,
    After the black storm, the eternal, beauteous bow!
Brother, to rosy-painted mists that arch beyond,
    Blithely I go.

My brows men laureled and my lyre
    Twined with immortal ivy for one little rippling song;
My "House of Golden Leaves" they praised and "passionate fire"—
    But, Friend, the way is long!

Onward and onward, up! away!
    Though Fear flaunt all his banners in my face,
And my feet stumble, lo! the Orphean Day!
    Forward by God's grace!

These signs are still before me: "Fear,"
    "Danger," "Unprecedented," and I hear black "No"
Still thundering, and "Churl." Good Friend, I rest me here—
    Then to the glittering bow!

Loometh and cometh Hate in wrath,
    Mailed Wrong, swart Servitude and Shame with bitter rue,
Nathless a Negro poet's feet must tread the path
    The winged god knew.

Thus, my true Brother, dream-led, I
    Forefend the anathema, following the span.
I hold my head as proudly high
    As any man.

     JAMES D. CORROTHERS

In the Matter of Two Men

One does such work as one will not,
    And well each knows the right;
Though the white storm howls, or the sun is hot,
    The black must serve the white.
And it's, oh, for the white man's softening flesh,
    While the black man's muscles grow!
Well I know which grows the mightier,
    I know; full well I know.

The white man seeks the soft, fat place,
    And he moves and he works by rule.
Ingenious grows the humbler race
    In Oppression's prodding school.
And it's, oh, for a white man gone to seed,
    While the Negro struggles so!
And I know which race develops most,
    I know; yes, well I know.

The white man rides in a palace car,
    And the Negro rides "Jim Crow."
To damn the other with bolt and bar,
    One creepeth so low; so low!
And it's, oh, for a master's nose in the mire,
    While the humbled hearts o'erflow!
Well I know whose soul grows big at this,
    And whose grows small; *I know*!

The white man leases out his land,
    And the Negro tills the same.
One works; one loafs and takes command;
    But I know who wins the game!
And it's, oh, for the white man's shrinking soil,
    As the black's rich acres grow!
Well I know how the signs point out at last,
    I know; ah, well I know!

The white man votes for his color's sake,
    While the black, for his is barred;
(Though "ignorance" is the charge they make),
    But the black man studies hard.
And it's, oh, for the white man's sad neglect,
    For the power of his light let go!
So, I know which man must win at last,
    I know! Ah, Friend, I know!

An Indignation Dinner

Dey was hard times jes fo' Christmas round our neighborhood one year;
So we held a secret meetin', whah de white folks couldn't hear,
To 'scuss de situation, an' to see what could be done
Towa'd a fust-class Christmas dinneh an' a little Christmas fun.

Rufus Green, who called de meetin', ris an' said: "In dis here town,
An' throughout de land, de white folks is a-tryin' to keep us down."
S' 'e: "Dey's bought us, sold us, beat us; now dey 'buse us 'ca'se we's
        free;
But when dey tetch my stomach, dey's done gone too fur foh me!

"Is I right?" "You sho is, Rufus!" roared a dozen hungry throats.
"Ef you'd keep a mule a-wo'kin', don't you tamper wid his oats.
Dat's sense," continued Rufus. "But dese white folks nowadays
Has done got so close and stingy you can't live on what dey pays.

"Here 'tis Christmas-time, an', folkses, I's indignant 'nough to choke.
Whah's our Christmas dinneh comin' when we's 'mos' completely
        broke?
I can't hahdly 'fo'd a toothpick an' a glass o' water. Mad?
Say, I'm desp'ret! Dey jes better treat me nice, dese white folks had!"

Well, dey 'bused de white folks scan'lous, till old Pappy Simmons ris,
Leanin' on his cane to s'pote him, on account his rheumatis',
An' s' 'e: "Chilun, whut's dat wintry wind a-sighin' th'ough de street
'Bout yo' wasted summeh wages? But, no matter, we mus' eat.

"Now, I seed a beau'ful tuhkey on a certain gemmun's fahm.
He's a-growin' fat an' sassy, an' a-struttin' to a chahm.
Chickens, sheeps, hogs, sweet pertaters—all de craps is fine dis year;
All we needs is a committee foh to tote de goodies here."

Well, we lit right in an' voted dat it was a gran idee,
An' de dinneh we had Christmas was worth trabblin' miles to see;
An' we eat a full an' plenty, big an' little, great an' small,
Not beca'se we was dishonest, but indignant, sah. Dat's all.

Dream and the Song

So oft our hearts, belovèd lute,
In blossomy haunts of song are mute;
So long we pore, 'mid murmurings dull,
O'er loveliness unutterable.
So vain is all our passion strong!
The dream is lovelier than the song.

The rose thought, touched by words, doth turn
Wan ashes. Still, from memory's urn,
The lingering blossoms tenderly
Refute our wilding minstrelsy.
Alas! we work but beauty's wrong!
The dream is lovelier than the song.

Yearned Shelley o'er the golden flame?
Left Keats for beauty's lure, a name
But "writ in water"? Woe is me!
To grieve o'er flowerful faëry.
My Phasian doves are flown so long—
The dream is lovelier than the song!

Ah, though we build a bower of dawn,
The golden-wingèd bird is gone,
And morn may gild, through shimmering leaves,
Only the swallow-twittering eaves.
What art may house or gold prolong
A dream far lovelier than a song?

The lilting witchery, the unrest
Of wingèd dreams, is in our breast;
But ever dear Fulfilment's eyes
Gaze otherward. The long-sought prize,
My lute, must to the gods belong.
The dream is lovelier than the song.

DANIEL WEBSTER DAVIS

'WEH DOWN SOUF

O, de birds ar' sweetly singin',
   'Weh down Souf,
An' de banjer is a-ringin',
   'Weh down Souf;
An' my heart it is a-sighin',
Whil' de moments am a-flyin',
Fur my hom' I am a-cryin',
   'Weh down Souf.

Dar de pickaninnies 's playin',
   'Weh down Souf,
An' fur dem I am a-prayin',
   'Weh down Souf;
An' when I gits sum munny,
Yo' kin bet I'm goin', my hunny,
Fur de lan' dat am so sunny,
   'Weh down Souf.

Whil' de win' up here's a-blowin',
   'Weh down Souf
De corn is sweetly growin',
   'Weh down Souf.
Dey tells me here ub freedum,
But I ain't a-gwine to heed um,
But I'se gwine fur to lebe um,
   Fur 'weh down Souf.

I bin up here a-wuckin',
   From 'weh down Souf,
An' I ain't a bin a-shurkin'—
   I'm frum 'weh down Souf;
But I'm gittin' mighty werry,
An' de days a-gittin' drerry,
An' I'm hongry, O, so berry,
   Fur my hom' down Souf.

O, de moon dar shines de brighter,
　　'Weh down Souf,
An' I know my heart is lighter,
　　'Weh down Souf;
An' de berry thought brings pledjur,
I'll be happy dar 'dout medjur,
Fur dar I hab my tredjur,
　　'Weh down Souf.

Hog Meat

Deze eatin' folks may tell me ub de gloriz ub spring lam',
An' de toofsumnis ub tuckey et wid cel'ry an' wid jam;
Ub beef-st'ak fried wid unyuns, an' sezoned up so fine—
But you' jes' kin gimme hog-meat, an' I'm happy all de time.

When de fros' is on de pun'kin an' de sno'-flakes in de ar',
I den begin rejoicin'—hog-killin' time is near;
An' de vizhuns ub de fucher den fill my nightly dreams,
Fur de time is fas' a-comin' fur de 'lishus pork an' beans.

We folks dat's frum de kuntry may be behin' de sun—
We don't like city eatin's, wid beefsteaks dat ain' done—
'Dough mutton chops is splendid, an' dem veal cutlits fine,
To me 'tain't like a sphar-rib, or gret big chunk ub chine.

Jes' talk to me 'bout hog-meat, ef yo' want to see me pleased,
Fur biled wid beans tiz gor'jus, or made in hog-head cheese;
An' I could jes' be happy, 'dout money, cloze or house,
Wid plenty yurz an' pig feet made in ol'-fashun "souse."

I 'fess I'm only humun, I hab my joys an' cares—
Sum days de clouds hang hebby, sum days de skies ar' fair;
But I forgib my in'miz, my heart is free frum hate,
When my bread is filled wid cracklins an' dar's chidlins on my plate.

'Dough 'possum meat is glo'yus wid 'taters in de pan,
But put 'longside pork sassage it takes a backward stan';
Ub all yer fancy eatin's, jes gib to me fur mine
Sum souse or pork or chidlins, sum sphar-rib, or de chine.

WILLIAM H.A. MOORE

Dusk Song

The garden is very quiet to-night,
The dusk has gone with the Evening Star,
And out on the bay a lone ship light
Makes a silver pathway over the bar
Where the sea sings low.

I follow the light with an earnest eye,
Creeping along to the thick far-away,
Until it fell in the depths of the deep, dark sky
With the haunting dream of the dusk of day
And its lovely glow.

Long nights, long nights and the whisperings of new ones,
Flame the line of the pathway down to the sea
With the halo of new dreams and the hallow of old ones,
And they bring magic light to my love reverie
And a lover's regret.

Tender sorrow for loss of a soft murmured word,
Tender measure of doubt in a faint, aching heart,
Tender listening for wind-songs in the tree heights heard
When you and I were of the dusks a part,
Are with me yet.

I pray for faith to the noble spirit of Space,
I sound the cosmic depths for the measure of glory
Which will bring to this earth the imperishable race
Of whom Beauty dreamed in the soul-toned story
The Prophets told.

Silence and love and deep wonder of stars
Dust-silver the heavens from west to east,
From south to north, and in a maze of bars
Invisible I wander far from the feast
As night grows old.

Half blind is my vision I know to the truth,
My ears are half deaf to the voice of the tear
That touches the silences as Autumn's ruth
Steals thru the dusks of each returning year
A goodly friend.

The Autumn, then Winter and wintertime's grief!
But the weight of the snow is the glistening gift
Which loving brings to the rose and its leaf,
For the days of the roses glow in the drift
And never end.

*　*　*　*　*

The moon has come. Wan and pallid is she.
The spell of half memories, the touch of half tears,
And the wounds of worn passions she brings to me
With all the tremor of the far-off years
And their mad wrong.

Yet the garden is very quiet to-night,
The dusk has long gone with the Evening Star,
And out on the bay the moon's wan light
Lays a silver pathway beyond the bar,
Dear heart, pale and long.

　　　　　WILLIAM H.A. MOORE

It Was Not Fate

It was not fate which overtook me,
Rather a wayward, wilful wind
That blew hot for awhile
And then, as the even shadows came, blew cold.
What pity it is that a man grown old in life's dreaming
Should stop, e'en for a moment, to look into a woman's eyes.
And I forgot!
Forgot that one's heart must be steeled against the east wind.
Life and death alike come out of the East:
Life as tender as young grass,
Death as dreadful as the sight of clotted blood.
I shall go back into the darkness,
Not to dream but to seek the light again.
I shall go by paths, mayhap,
On roads that wind around the foothills
Where the plains are bare and wild
And the passers-by come few and far between.
I want the night to be long, the moon blind,
The hills thick with moving memories,
And my heart beating a breathless requiem
For all the dead days I have lived.
When the Dawn comes—Dawn, deathless, dreaming—
I shall will that my soul must be cleansed of hate,
I shall pray for strength to hold children close to my heart,
I shall desire to build houses where the poor will know shelter,
    comfort, beauty.
And then may I look into a woman's eyes
And find holiness, love and the peace which passeth understanding.

W.E. BURGHARDT DU BOIS

A Litany of Atlanta

Done at Atlanta, in the Day of Death, 1906

O Silent God, Thou whose voice afar in mist and mystery hath left
our ears an-hungered in these fearful days—
Hear us, good Lord!

Listen to us, Thy children: our faces dark with doubt are made a
mockery in Thy sanctuary. With uplifted hands we front Thy
heaven, O God, crying:
We beseech Thee to hear us, good Lord!

We are not better than our fellows, Lord, we are but weak and human
men. When our devils do deviltry, curse Thou the doer and the
deed: curse them as we curse them, do to them all and more than
ever they have done to innocence and weakness, to womanhood
and home.
Have mercy upon us, miserable sinners!

And yet whose is the deeper guilt? Who made these devils? Who
nursed them in crime and fed them on injustice? Who ravished and
debauched their mothers and their grandmothers? Who bought
and sold their crime, and waxed fat and rich on public iniquity?
Thou knowest, good God!

Is this Thy justice, O Father, that guile be easier than innocence, and
the innocent crucified for the guilt of the untouched guilty?
Justice, O judge of men!

Wherefore do we pray? Is not the God of the fathers dead? Have not
seers seen in Heaven's halls Thine hearsed and lifeless form stark
amidst the black and rolling smoke of sin, where all along bow
bitter forms of endless dead?
Awake, Thou that sleepest!

Thou art not dead, but flown afar, up hills of endless light, thru blazing
corridors of suns, where worlds do swing of good and gentle men,

of women strong and free—far from the cozenage, black hypocrisy and chaste prostitution of this shameful speck of dust!
Turn again, O Lord, leave us not to perish in our sin!

From lust of body and lust of blood
Great God, deliver us!

From lust of power and lust of gold,
Great God, deliver us!

From the leagued lying of despot and of brute,
Great God, deliver us!

A city lay in travail, God our Lord, and from her loins sprang twin Murder and Black Hate. Red was the midnight; clang, crack and cry of death and fury filled the air and trembled underneath the stars when church spires pointed silently to Thee. And all this was to sate the greed of greedy men who hide behind the veil of vengeance!
Bend us Thine ear, O Lord!

In the pale, still morning we looked upon the deed. We stopped our ears and held our leaping hands, but they—did they not wag their heads and leer and cry with bloody jaws: *Cease from Crime!* The word was mockery, for thus they train a hundred crimes while we do cure one.
Turn again our captivity, O Lord!

Behold this maimed and broken thing; dear God, it was an humble black man who toiled and sweat to save a bit from the pittance paid him. They told him: *Work and Rise.* He worked. Did this man sin? Nay, but some one told how some one said another did—one whom he had never seen nor known. Yet for that man's crime this man lieth maimed and murdered, his wife naked to shame, his children, to poverty and evil.
Hear us, O Heavenly Father!

Doth not this justice of hell stink in Thy nostrils, O God? How long shall the mounting flood of innocent blood roar in Thine ears and

pound in our hearts for vengeance? Pile the pale frenzy of blood-crazed brutes who do such deeds high on Thine altar, Jehovah Jireh, and burn it in hell forever and forever!
Forgive us, good Lord; we know not what we say!

Bewildered we are, and passion-tost, mad with the madness of a mobbed and mocked and murdered people; straining at the armposts of Thy Throne, we raise our shackled hands and charge Thee, God, by the bones of our stolen fathers, by the tears of our dead mothers, by the very blood of Thy crucified Christ: *What meaneth this?* Tell us the Plan; give us the Sign!
Keep not thou silence, O God!

Sit no longer blind, Lord God, deaf to our prayer and dumb to our dumb suffering. Surely Thou too art not white, O Lord, a pale, bloodless, heartless thing?
Ah! Christ of all the Pities!

Forgive the thought! Forgive these wild, blasphemous words. Thou art still the God of our black fathers, and in Thy soul's soul sit some soft darkenings of the evening, some shadowings of the velvet night.

But whisper—speak—call, great God, for Thy silence is white terror to our hearts! The way, O God, show us the way and point us the path.

Whither? North is greed and South is blood; within, the coward, and without, the liar. Whither? To death?
Amen! Welcome dark sleep!

Whither? To life? But not this life, dear God, not this. Let the cup pass from us, tempt us not beyond our strength, for there is that clamoring and clawing within, to whose voice we would not listen, yet shudder lest we must, and it is red, Ah! God! It is a red and awful shape.
Selah!

In yonder East trembles a star.
Vengeance is mine; I will repay, saith the Lord!

Thy will, O Lord, be done!
  Kyrie Eleison!

Lord, we have done these pleading, wavering words.
  We beseech Thee to hear us, good Lord!

We bow our heads and hearken soft to the sobbing of women and
  little children.
  We beseech Thee to hear us, good Lord!

Our voices sink in silence and in night.
  Hear us, good Lord!

In night, O God of a godless land!
  Amen!

In silence, O Silent God.
  Selah!

GEORGE MARION MCCLELLAN

Dogwood Blossoms

To dreamy languors and the violet mist
    Of early Spring, the deep sequestered vale
Gives first her paling-blue Miamimist,
    Where blithely pours the cuckoo's annual tale
Of Summer promises and tender green,
    Of a new life and beauty yet unseen.
The forest trees have yet a sighing mouth,
    Where dying winds of March their branches swing,
While upward from the dreamy, sunny South,
    A hand invisible leads on the Spring.

His rounds from bloom to bloom the bee begins
    With flying song, and cowslip wine he sups,
Where to the warm and passing southern winds,
    Azaleas gently swing their yellow cups.
Soon everywhere, with glory through and through,
    The fields will spread with every brilliant hue.
But high o'er all the early floral train,
    Where softness all the arching sky resumes,
The dogwood dancing to the winds' refrain,
    In stainless glory spreads its snowy blooms.

A Butterfly in Church

What dost thou here, thou shining, sinless thing,
With many colored hues and shapely wing?
Why quit the open field and summer air
To flutter here? Thou hast no need of prayer.

'Tis meet that we, who this great structure built,
Should come to be redeemed and washed from guilt,
For we this gilded edifice within
Are come, with erring hearts and stains of sin.

But thou art free from guilt as God on high;
Go, seek the blooming waste and open sky,
And leave us here our secret woes to bear,
Confessionals and agonies of prayer.

THE HILLS OF SEWANEE

Sewanee Hills of dear delight,
    Prompting my dreams that used to be,
I know you are waiting me still to-night
    By the Unika Range of Tennessee.

The blinking stars in endless space,
    The broad moonlight and silvery gleams,
To-night caress your wind-swept face,
    And fold you in a thousand dreams.

Your far outlines, less seen than felt,
    Which wind with hill propensities,
In moonlight dreams I see you melt
    Away in vague immensities.

And, far away, I still can feel
    Your mystery that ever speaks
Of vanished things, as shadows steal
    Across your breast and rugged peaks.

O, dear blue hills, that lie apart,
    And wait so patiently down there,
Your peace takes hold upon my heart
    And makes its burden less to bear.

THE FEET OF JUDAS

Christ washed the feet of Judas!
The dark and evil passions of his soul,
His secret plot, and sordidness complete,
His hate, his purposing, Christ knew the whole,
And still in love he stooped and washed his feet.

Christ washed the feet of Judas!
Yet all his lurking sin was bare to him,
His bargain with the priest, and more than this,
In Olivet, beneath the moonlight dim,
Aforehand knew and felt his treacherous kiss.

Christ washed the feet of Judas!
And so ineffable his love 'twas meet,
That pity fill his great forgiving heart,
And tenderly to wash the traitor's feet,
Who in his Lord had basely sold his part.

Christ washed the feet of Judas!
And thus a girded servant, self-abased,
Taught that no wrong this side the gate of heaven
Was ever too great to wholly be effaced,
And though unasked, in spirit be forgiven.

And so if we have ever felt the wrong
Of Trampled rights, of caste, it matters not,
What e'er the soul has felt or suffered long,
Oh, heart! this one thing should not be forgot:
Christ washed the feet of Judas.

GEORGE MARION MCCLELLAN

WILLIAM STANLEY BRAITHWAITE

SANDY STAR AND WILLIE GEE

Sandy Star and Willie Gee,
Count 'em two, you make 'em three:
Pluck the man and boy apart
And you'll see into my heart.

SANDY STAR

I

Sculptured Worship

The zones of warmth around his heart,
    No alien airs had crossed;
But he awoke one morn to feel
    The magic numbness of autumnal frost.

His thoughts were a loose skein of threads,
    And tangled emotions, vague and dim;
And sacrificing what he loved
    He lost the dearest part of him.

In sculptured worship now he lives,
    His one desire a prisoned ache;
If he can never melt again
    His very heart will break.

II

Laughing It Out

He had a whim and laughed it out
    Upon the exit of a chance;
He floundered in a sea of doubt—
    If life was real—or just romance.

Sometimes upon his brow would come
    A little pucker of defiance;
He totalled in a word the sum
    Of all man made of facts and science.

And then a hearty laugh would break,
    A reassuring shrug of shoulder;
And we would from his fancy take
    A faith in death which made life bolder.

WILLIAM STANLEY BRAITHWAITE

III

Exit

No, his exit by the gate
    Will not leave the wind ajar;
He will go when it is late
    With a misty star.

One will call, he cannot see;
    One will call, he will not hear;
He will take no company
    Nor a hope or fear.

We shall smile who loved him so—
    They who gave him hate will weep;
But for us the winds will blow
    Pulsing through his sleep.

IV

The Way

He could not tell the way he came,
    Because his chart was lost:
Yet all his way was paved with flame
    From the bourne he crossed.

He did not know the way to go,
    Because he had no map:
He followed where the winds blow,—
    And the April sap.

He never knew upon his brow
    The secret that he bore,—
And laughs away the mystery now
    The dark's at his door.

V

Onus Probandi

No more from out the sunset,
    No more across the foam,
No more across the windy hills
    Will Sandy Star come home.

He went away to search it
    With a curse upon his tongue:
And in his hand the staff of life,
    Made music as it swung.

I wonder if he found it,
    And knows the mystery now—
Our Sandy Star who went away,
    With the secret on his brow.

WILLIAM STANLEY BRAITHWAITE

DEL CASCAR

Del Cascar, Del Cascar,
Stood upon a flaming star,
Stood, and let his feet hang down
Till in China the toes turned brown.

And he reached his fingers over
The rim of the sea, like sails from Dover,
And caught a Mandarin at prayer,
And tickled his nose in Orion's hair.

The sun went down through crimson bars,
And left his blind face battered with stars—
But the brown toes in China kept
Hot the tears Del Cascar wept.

Turn Me to My Yellow Leaves

Turn me to my yellow leaves,
I am better satisfied;
There is something in me grieves—
That was never born, and died.
Let me be a scarlet flame
On a windy autumn morn,
I who never had a name,
Nor from breathing image born.
From the margin let me fall
Where the farthest stars sink down,
And the void consumes me,—all
In nothingness to drown.
Let me dream my dream entire,
Withered as an autumn leaf—
Let me have my vain desire,
Vain—as it is brief.

WILLIAM STANLEY BRAITHWAITE

Ironic: LL.D.

There are no hollows any more
Between the mountains; the prairie floor
Is like a curtain with the drape
Of the winds' invisible shape;
And nowhere seen and nowhere heard
The sea's quiet as a sleeping bird.

Now we're traveling, what holds back
Arrival, in the very track
Where the urge put forth; so we stay
And move a thousand miles a day.
Time's a Fancy ringing bells
Whose meaning, charlatan history, tells!

Scintilla

I kissed a kiss in youth
    Upon a dead man's brow;
And that was long ago,—
    And I'm a grown man now.

It's lain there in the dust,
    Thirty years and more;—
My lips that set a light
    At a dead man's door.

WILLIAM STANLEY BRAITHWAITE

Sic Vita

Heart free, hand free,
    Blue above, brown under,
All the world to me
    Is a place of wonder.
Sun shine, moon shine,
    Stars, and winds a-blowing,
All into this heart of mine
    Flowing, flowing, flowing!

Mind free, step free,
    Days to follow after,
Joys of life sold to me
    For the price of laughter.
Girl's love, man's love,
    Love of work and duty,
Just a will of God's to prove
    Beauty, beauty, beauty!

Rhapsody

I am glad daylong for the gift of song,
For time and change and sorrow;
For the sunset wings and the world-end things
Which hang on the edge of to-morrow.
I am glad for my heart whose gates apart
Are the entrance-place of wonders,
Where dreams come in from the rush and din
Like sheep from the rains and thunders.

GEORGE REGINALD MARGETSON

Stanzas from the Fledgling Bard and the Poetry Society

Part I

I'm out to find the new, the modern school,
Where Science trains the fledgling bard to fly,
Where critics teach the ignorant, the fool,
To write the stuff the editors would buy;
It matters not e'en tho it be a lie,—
Just so it aims to smash tradition's crown
And build up one instead decked with a new renown.

A thought is haunting me by night and day,
And in some safe archive I seek to lay it;
I have some startling thing I wish to say,
And they can put me wise just how to say it.
Without their aid, I, like the ass, must bray it,
Without due knowledge of its mood and tense,
And so 'tis sure to fail the bard to recompense.

Will some kind one direct me to that college
Where every budding genius now is headed,
The only source to gain poetic knowledge,
Where all the sacred truths lay deep imbedded,
Where nothing but the genuine goods are shredded,—
The factory where they shape new feet and meters
That make poetic symbols sound like carpet beaters.

*   *   *   *   *

I hope I'll be an eligible student,
E'en tho I am no poet in a sense,
But just a hot-head youth with ways imprudent,—
A rustic ranting rhymer like by chance
Who thinks that he can make the muses dance
By beating on some poet's borrowed lyre,
To win some fool's applause and please his own desire.

Perhaps they'll never know or e'en suspect
That I am not a true, a genuine poet;
If in the poet's colors I am decked
They may not ask me e'er to prove or show it.
I'll play the wise old cock, nor try to crow it,
But be content to gaze with open mind;
I'll never show the lead but eye things from behind.

Part II

I have a problem all alone to solve,
A problem how to find the poetry club,
It makes my sky piece like a top revolve,
For fear that they might mark me for a snob.
They'll call me poetry monger and then dub
Me rustic rhymer, anything they choose,
Ay, anything at all, but heaven's immortal muse.

Great Byron, when he published his Childe book,
In which he sang of all his lovely dears,
Called forth hot condemnation and cold look,
From lesser mortals who were not his peers.
They chided him for telling his affairs,
Because they could not tell their own so well,
They plagued the poet lord and made his life a hell.

They called him lewd, vile drunkard, vicious wight,
And all because he dared to tell the truth,
Because he was no cursed hermaphrodite,—
A full fledged genius with the fire of youth.
They hounded him, they hammered him forsooth;
Because he blended human with divine,
They branded him "the bard of women and of wine."

Of course I soak the booze once in a while,
But I don't wake the town to sing and shout it;
I love the girls, they win me with a smile,
But no one knows, for I won't write about it.
And so the fools may never think to doubt it,

GEORGE REGINALD MARGETSON

When I declare I am a moral man,
As gifted, yet as good as God did ever plan.

*   *   *   *   *

Every man has got a hobby,
Every poet has some fault,
Every sweet contains its bitter,
Every fresh thing has its salt.

Every mountain has a valley,
Every valley has a hill,
Every ravine is a river,
Every river is a rill.

Every fool has got some wisdom,
Every wise man is a fool,
Every scholar is a block-head,
Every dunce has been to school.

Every bad man is a good man,
Every fat man is not stout,
Every good man is a bad man
But 'tis hard to find him out.

Every strong man is a weak man,
You may doubt it as you please,
Every well man is a sick man,
Every doctor has disease.

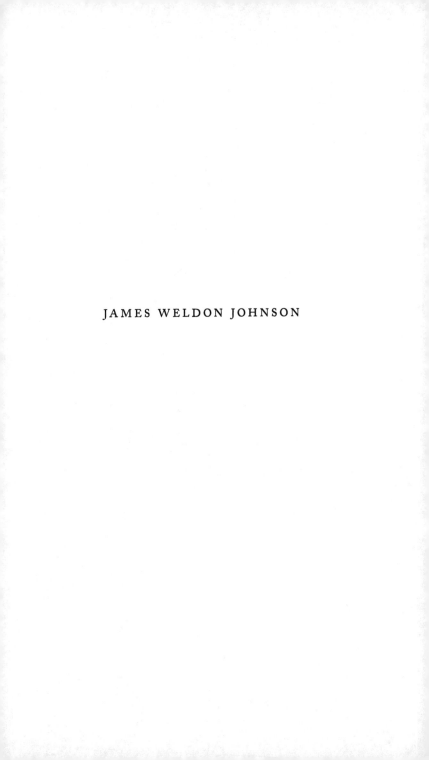

JAMES WELDON JOHNSON

O Black and Unknown Bards

O black and unknown bards of long ago,
How came your lips to touch the sacred fire?
How, in your darkness, did you come to know
The power and beauty of the minstrel's lyre?
Who first from midst his bonds lifted his eyes?
Who first from out the still watch, lone and long,
Feeling the ancient faith of prophets rise
Within his dark-kept soul, burst into song?

Heart of what slave poured out such melody
As "Steal away to Jesus"? On its strains
His spirit must have nightly floated free,
Though still about his hands he felt his chains.
Who heard great "Jordan roll"? Whose starward eye
Saw chariot "swing low"? And who was he
That breathed that comforting, melodic sigh,
"Nobody knows de trouble I see"?

What merely living clod, what captive thing,
Could up toward God through all its darkness grope,
And find within its deadened heart to sing
These songs of sorrow, love and faith, and hope?
How did it catch that subtle undertone,
That note in music heard not with the ears?
How sound the elusive reed so seldom blown,
Which stirs the soul or melts the heart to tears.

Not that great German master in his dream
Of harmonies that thundered amongst the stars
At the creation, ever heard a theme
Nobler than "Go down, Moses." Mark its bars
How like a mighty trumpet-call they stir
The blood. Such are the notes that men have sung
Going to valorous deeds; such tones there were
That helped make history when Time was young.

There is a wide, wide wonder in it all,
That from degraded rest and servile toil
The fiery spirit of the seer should call
These simple children of the sun and soil.
O black slave singers, gone, forgot, unfamed,
You—you alone, of all the long, long line
Of those who've sung untaught, unknown, unnamed,
Have stretched out upward, seeking the divine.

You sang not deeds of heroes or of kings;
No chant of bloody war, no exulting pean
Of arms-won triumphs; but your humble strings
You touched in chord with music empyrean.
You sang far better than you knew; the songs
That for your listeners' hungry hearts sufficed
Still live,—but more than this to you belongs:
You sang a race from wood and stone to Christ.

JAMES WELDON JOHNSON

Sence You Went Away

Seems lak to me de stars don't shine so bright,
Seems lak to me de sun done loss his light,
Seems lak to me der's nothin' goin' right,
    Sence you went away.

Seems lak to me de sky ain't half so blue,
Seems lak to me dat ev'ything wants you,
Seems lak to me I don't know what to do,
    Sence you went away.

Seems lak to me dat ev'ything is wrong,
Seems lak to me de day's jes twice es long,
Seems lak to me de bird's forgot his song,
    Sence you went away.

Seems lak to me I jes can't he'p but sigh,
Seems lak to me ma th'oat keeps gittin' dry,
Seems lak to me a tear stays in ma eye,
    Sence you went away.

THE CREATION

(A Negro Sermon)

And God stepped out on space,
And He looked around and said,
   "I'm lonely—
I'll make me a world."

And far as the eye of God could see
Darkness covered everything,
Blacker than a hundred midnights
Down in a cypress swamp.

Then God smiled,
And the light broke,
And the darkness rolled up on one side,
And the light stood shining on the other,
And God said, *"That's good!"*

Then God reached out and took the light in His hands,
And God rolled the light around in His hands
Until He made the sun;
And He set that sun a-blazing in the heavens.
And the light that was left from making the sun
God gathered it up in a shining ball
And flung it against the darkness,
Spangling the night with the moon and stars.
Then down between
The darkness and the light
He hurled the world;
And God said, *"That's good!"*

Then God himself stepped down—
And the sun was on His right hand,
And the moon was on His left;
The stars were clustered about His head,
And the earth was under His feet.

And God walked, and where He trod
His footsteps hollowed the valleys out
And bulged the mountains up.

Then He stopped and looked and saw
That the earth was hot and barren.
So God stepped over to the edge of the world
And He spat out the seven seas;
He batted His eyes, and the lightnings flashed;
He clapped His hands, and the thunders rolled;
And the waters above the earth came down,
The cooling waters came down.

Then the green grass sprouted,
And the little red flowers blossomed,
The pine tree pointed his finger to the sky,
And the oak spread out his arms,
The lakes cuddled down in the hollows of the ground,
And the rivers ran down to the sea;
And God smiled again,
And the rainbow appeared,
And curled itself around His shoulder.

Then God raised His arm and He waved His hand
Over the sea and over the land,
And He said, *"Bring forth! Bring forth!"*
And quicker than God could drop His hand,
Fishes and fowls
And beasts and birds
Swam the rivers and the seas,
Roamed the forests and the woods,
And split the air with their wings.
And God said, *"That's good!"*

Then God walked around,
And God looked around
On all that He had made.
He looked at His sun,
And He looked at His moon,

'And He looked at His little stars;
He looked on His world
With all its living things,
And God said, *"I'm lonely still."*

Then God sat down
On the side of a hill where He could think;
By a deep, wide river He sat down;
With His head in His hands,
God thought and thought,
Till He thought, *"I'll make me a man!"*

Up from the bed of the river
God scooped the clay;
And by the bank of the river
He kneeled Him down;
And there the great God Almighty
Who lit the sun and fixed it in the sky,
Who flung the stars to the most far corner of the night,
Who rounded the earth in the middle of His hand;
This Great God,
Like a mammy bending over her baby,
Kneeled down in the dust
Toiling over a lump of clay
Till He shaped it in His own image;

Then into it He blew the breath of life,
And man became a living soul.
Amen. Amen.

JAMES WELDON JOHNSON

The White Witch

O brothers mine, take care! Take care!
The great white witch rides out to-night.
Trust not your prowess nor your strength,
Your only safety lies in flight;
For in her glance there is a snare,
And in her smile there is a blight.

The great white witch you have not seen?
Then, younger brothers mine, forsooth,
Like nursery children you have looked
For ancient hag and snaggle-tooth;
But no, not so; the witch appears
In all the glowing charms of youth.

Her lips are like carnations, red,
Her face like new-born lilies, fair,
Her eyes like ocean waters, blue,
She moves with subtle grace and air,
And all about her head there floats
The golden glory of her hair.

But though she always thus appears
In form of youth and mood of mirth,
Unnumbered centuries are hers,
The infant planets saw her birth;
The child of throbbing Life is she,
Twin sister to the greedy earth.

And back behind those smiling lips,
And down within those laughing eyes,
And underneath the soft caress
Of hand and voice and purring sighs,
The shadow of the panther lurks,
The spirit of the vampire lies.

For I have seen the great white witch,
And she has led me to her lair,
And I have kissed her red, red lips
And cruel face so white and fair;
Around me she has twined her arms,
And bound me with her yellow hair.

I felt those red lips burn and sear
My body like a living coal;
Obeyed the power of those eyes
As the needle trembles to the pole;
And did not care although I felt
The strength go ebbing from my soul.

Oh! she has seen your strong young limbs,
And heard your laughter loud and gay,
And in your voices she has caught
The echo of a far-off day,
When man was closer to the earth;
And she has marked you for her prey.

She feels the old Antaean strength
In you, the great dynamic beat
Of primal passions, and she sees
In you the last besieged retreat
Of love relentless, lusty, fierce,
Love pain-ecstatic, cruel-sweet.

O, brothers mine, take care! Take care!
The great white witch rides out to-night.
O, younger brothers mine, beware!
Look not upon her beauty bright;
For in her glance there is a snare,
And in her smile there is a blight.

JAMES WELDON JOHNSON

Mother Night

Eternities before the first-born day,
  Or ere the first sun fledged his wings of flame,
  Calm Night, the everlasting and the same,
  A brooding mother over chaos lay.
And whirling suns shall blaze and then decay,
  Shall run their fiery courses and then claim
  The haven of the darkness whence they came;
  Back to Nirvanic peace shall grope their way.

So when my feeble sun of life burns out,
  And sounded is the hour for my long sleep,
  I shall, full weary of the feverish light,
Welcome the darkness without fear or doubt,
  And heavy-lidded, I shall softly creep
  Into the quiet bosom of the Night.

O Southland!

O Southland! O Southland!
    Have you not heard the call,
The trumpet blown, the word made known
    To the nations, one and all?
The watchword, the hope-word,
    Salvation's present plan?
A gospel new, for all—for you:
    Man shall be saved by man.

O Southland! O Southland!
    Do you not hear to-day
The mighty beat of onward feet,
    And know you not their way?
'Tis forward, 'tis upward,
    On to the fair white arch
Of Freedom's dome, and there is room
    For each man who would march.

O Southland, fair Southland!
    Then why do you still cling
To an idle age and a musty page,
    To a dead and useless thing?
'Tis springtime! 'Tis work-time!
    The world is young again!
And God's above, and God is love,
    And men are only men.

O Southland! my Southland!
    O birthland! do not shirk
The toilsome task, nor respite ask,
    But gird you for the work.
Remember, remember
    That weakness stalks in pride;
That he is strong who helps along
    The faint one at his side.

JAMES WELDON JOHNSON

Brothers

See! There he stands; not brave, but with an air
Of sullen stupor. Mark him well! Is he
Not more like brute than man? Look in his eye!
No light is there; none, save the glint that shines
In the now glaring, and now shifting orbs
Of some wild animal caught in the hunter's trap.

How came this beast in human shape and form?
Speak, man!—We call you man because you wear
His shape—How are you thus? Are you not from
That docile, child-like, tender-hearted race
Which we have known three centuries? Not from
That more than faithful race which through three wars
Fed our dear wives and nursed our helpless babes
Without a single breach of trust? Speak out!

I am, and am not.

Then who, why are you?

I am a thing not new, I am as old
As human nature. I am that which lurks,
Ready to spring whenever a bar is loosed;
The ancient trait which fights incessantly
Against restraint, balks at the upward climb;
The weight forever seeking to obey
The law of downward pull;—and I am more:
The bitter fruit am I of planted seed;
The resultant, the inevitable end
Of evil forces and the powers of wrong.

Lessons in degradation, taught and learned,
The memories of cruel sights and deeds,
The pent-up bitterness, the unspent hate
Filtered through fifteen generations have

Sprung up and found in me sporadic life.
In me the muttered curse of dying men,
On me the stain of conquered women, and
Consuming me the fearful fires of lust,
Lit long ago, by other hands than mine.
In me the down-crushed spirit, the hurled-back prayers
Of wretches now long dead,—their dire bequests,—
In me the echo of the stifled cry
Of children for their bartered mothers' breasts.

     I claim no race, no race claims me; I am
No more than human dregs; degenerate;
The monstrous offspring of the monster, Sin;
I am—just what I am. . . The race that fed
Your wives and nursed your babes would do the same
To-day, but I—
          Enough, the brute must die!
Quick! Chain him to that oak! It will resist
The fire much longer than this slender pine.
Now bring the fuel! Pile it'round him! Wait!
Pile not so fast or high! or we shall lose
The agony and terror in his face.

And now the torch! Good fuel that! the flames
Already leap head-high. Ha! hear that shriek!
And there's another! Wilder than the first.
Fetch water! Water! Pour a little on

The fire, lest it should burn too fast. Hold so!
Now let it slowly blaze again. See there!
He squirms! He groans! His eyes bulge wildly out,
Searching around in vain appeal for help!
Another shriek, the last! Watch how the flesh
Grows crisp and hangs till, turned to ash, it sifts
Down through the coils of chain that hold erect
The ghastly frame against the bark-scorched tree.

                    JAMES WELDON JOHNSON

Stop! to each man no more than one man's share.
You take that bone, and you this tooth; the chain—
Let us divide its links; this skull, of course,
In fair division, to the leader comes.

And now his fiendish crime has been avenged;
Let us back to our wives and children.—Say,
What did he mean by those last muttered words,
"Brothers in spirit, brothers in deed are we"?

FIFTY YEARS (1863–1913)

On the Fiftieth Anniversary of the Signing of the Emancipation Proclamation.

O brothers mine, to-day we stand
    Where half a century sweeps our ken,
Since God, through Lincoln's ready hand,
    Struck off our bonds and made us men.

Just fifty years—a winter's day—
    As runs the history of a race;
Yet, as we look back o'er the way,
    How distant seems our starting place!

Look farther back! Three centuries!
    To where a naked, shivering score,
Snatched from their haunts across the seas,
    Stood, wild-eyed, on Virginia's shore.

This land is ours by right of birth,
    This land is ours by right of toil;
We helped to turn its virgin earth,
    Our sweat is in its fruitful soil.

Where once the tangled forest stood,—
    Where flourished once rank weed and thorn,—
Behold the path-traced, peaceful wood,
    The cotton white, the yellow corn.

To gain these fruits that have been earned,
    To hold these fields that have been won,
Our arms have strained, our backs have burned,
    Bent bare beneath a ruthless sun.

That Banner which is now the type
    Of victory on field and flood—
Remember, its first crimson stripe
    Was dyed by Attucks' willing blood.

JAMES WELDON JOHNSON

And never yet has come the cry—
    When that fair flag has been assailed—
For men to do, for men to die,
    That we have faltered or have failed.

We've helped to bear it, rent and torn,
    Through many a hot-breath'd battle breeze
Held in our hands, it has been borne
    And planted far across the seas.

And never yet,—O haughty Land,
    Let us, at least, for this be praised—
Has one black, treason-guided hand
    Ever against that flag been raised.

Then should we speak but servile words,
    Or shall we hang our heads in shame?
Stand back of new-come foreign hordes,
    And fear our heritage to claim?

No! stand erect and without fear,
    And for our foes let this suffice—
We've bought a rightful sonship here,
    And we have more than paid the price.

And yet, my brothers, well I know
    The tethered feet, the pinioned wings,
The spirit bowed beneath the blow,
    The heart grown faint from wounds and stings;

The staggering force of brutish might,
    That strikes and leaves us stunned and dazed;
The long, vain waiting through the night
    To hear some voice for justice raised.

Full well I know the hour when hope
    Sinks dead, and 'round us everywhere
Hangs stifling darkness, and we grope
    With hands uplifted in despair.

Courage! Look out, beyond, and see
    The far horizon's beckoning span!
Faith in your God-known destiny!
    We are a part of some great plan.

Because the tongues of Garrison
    And Phillips now are cold in death,
Think you their work can be undone?
    Or quenched the fires lit by their breath?

Think you that John Brown's spirit stops?
    That Lovejoy was but idly slain?
Or do you think those precious drops
    From Lincoln's heart were shed in vain?

That for which millions prayed and sighed,
    That for which tens of thousands fought,
For which so many freely died,
    God cannot let it come to naught.

JOHN WESLEY HOLLOWAY

MISS MELERLEE

Hello dar, Miss Melerlee!
Oh, you're pretty sight to see!
Sof brown cheek, an' smilin' face,
An' willowy form chuck full o' grace—
De sweetes' gal Ah evah see,
An' Ah wush dat you would marry me!
    Hello, Miss Melerlee!

Hello dar, Miss Melerlee!
You're de berry gal fo' me!
Pearly teef, an' shinin' hair,
An' silky arm so plump an' bare!
Ah lak yo' walk, Ah lak yo' clothes,
An' de way Ah love you,—goodness knows!
    Hello, Miss Melerlee!

Hello dar, Miss Melerlee!
Dat's not yo' name, but it ought to be!
Ah nevah seed yo' face befo'
An' lakly won't again no mo';
But yo' sweet smile will follow me
Cla'r into eternity!
    Farewell, Miss Melerlee!

CALLING THE DOCTOR

Ah'm sick, doctor-man, Ah'm sick!
Gi' me some'n' to he'p me quick,
    Don't,—Ah'll die!

Tried mighty hard fo' to cure mahse'f;
Tried all dem t'ings on de pantry she'f;
Couldn' fin' not'in' a-tall would do,
    An' so Ah sent fo' you.

"Wha'd Ah take?" Well, le' me see:
Firs',—horhound drops an' catnip tea;
Den rock candy soaked in rum,
An' a good sized chunk o' camphor gum;
Next Ah tried was castor oil,
An' snakeroot tea brought to a boil;

Sassafras tea fo' to clean mah blood;
But none o' dem t'ings didn' do no good.
Den when home remedies seem to shirk,
Dem pantry bottles was put to work:

Blue-mass, laud'num, liver pills,
"Sixty-six, fo' fever an' chills,"
Ready Relief, an' A.B.C.,
An' half a bottle of X.Y.Z.
An' sev'al mo' Ah don't recall,
Dey nevah done no good at all.

Mah appetite begun to fail;
'Ah fo'ced some clabber, about a pail,
Fo' mah ol' gran'ma always said
When yo' can't eat you're almost dead.

JOHN WESLEY HOLLOWAY

So Ah got scared an' sent for you.—
Now, doctor, see what you c'n do.
Ah'm sick, doctor-man. Gawd knows Ah'm sick!
Gi' me some'n' to he'p me quick,
    Don't,—Ah'll die!

The Corn Song

Jes' beyan a clump o' pines,—
    Lis'n to 'im now!—
Hyah de jolly black boy,
    Singin', at his plow!
In de early mornin',
    Thoo de hazy air,
Loud an' clear, sweet an' strong
    Comes de music rare:

    "O mah dovee, Who-ah!
    Do you love me? Who-ah!
        Who-ah!"
    An' as 'e tu'ns de cotton row,
    Hyah 'im tell 'is ol' mule so;
      "Whoa! Har! Come'ere!"

Don't yo' love a co'n song?
    How it stirs yo' blood!
Ever'body list'nin',
    In de neighborhood!
Standin' in yo' front do'
    In de misty mo'n,
Hyah de jolly black boy,
    Singin' in de co'n:

    "O Miss Julie, Who-ah!
    Love me truly, Who-ah!
        Who-ah!"
    Hyah 'im scol' 'is mule so,
    W'en 'e try to mek 'im go:
      "Gee! Whoa! Come 'ere!"

O you jolly black boy,
    Yod'lin' in de co'n,
Callin' to yo' dawlin',
    In de dewy mo'n,

Love 'er, boy, forevah,
　　Yodel ever' day;
Only le' me lis'n,
　　As yo' sing away:

　　"O mah dawlin'! Who-ah!
　　Hyah me callin'! Who-ah!
　　　　Who-ah!"
　　Tu'n aroun' anothah row,
　　Holler to yo' mule so:
　　"Whoa! Har! Come 'ere!"

BLACK MAMMIES

If Ah evah git to glory, an' Ah hope to mek it thoo,
Ah expec' to hyah a story, an' Ah hope you'll hyah it, too,—
Hit'll kiver Maine to Texas, an' f'om Bosting to Miami,—
Ov de highes' shaf in glory, 'rected to de Negro Mammy.

You will see a lot o' Washington, an' Washington again;
An' good ol' Fathah Lincoln, tow'rin' 'bove de rest o' men;
But dar'll be a bunch o' women standin' hard up by de th'one,
An' dey'll all be black an' homely,—'less de Virgin Mary's one.

Dey will be de talk of angels, dey will be de praise o' men,
An' de whi' folks would go crazy 'thout their Mammy folks again:
If it's r'ally true dat meekness makes you heir to all de eart',
Den our blessed, good ol' Mammies must 'a' been of noble birt'.

If de greates' is de servant, den Ah got to say o' dem,
Dey'll be standin' nex' to Jesus, sub to no one else but Him;
If de crown goes to de fait'ful, an' de palm de victors wear,
Dey'll be loaded down wid jewels more dan anybody dere.

She'd de hardes' road to trabel evah mortal had to pull;
But she knelt down in huh cabin till huh cup o' joy was full;
Dough' ol' Satan tried to shake huh f'om huh knees wid scowl an'
    frown,
She jes' "clumb up Jacob's ladder," an' he nevah drug huh down.

She'd jes' croon above de babies, she'd jes' sing when t'ings went
    wrong,
An' no matter what de trouble, she would meet it wid a song;
She jes' prayed huh way to heaben, findin' comfort in de rod;
She jes' "stole away to Jesus," she jes' sung huh way to God!

She "kep' lookin' ovah Jurdan," kep' "a-trustin' in de word,"
Kep' a-lookin' fo "de char'et," kep' "a-waitin' fo' de Lawd,"
If she evah had to quavah of de shadder of a doubt,
It ain't nevah been discovahed, fo' she nevah sung it out;

JOHN WESLEY HOLLOWAY

But she trusted in de shadder, an' she trusted in de shine,
An' she longed fo' one possession: "dat heaben to be mine";
An' she prayed huh chil'en freedom, but she won huhse'f de bes',—
Peace on eart' amids' huh sorrows, an' up yonder heabenly res'!

JOHN WESLEY HOLLOWAY

LESLIE PINCKNEY HILL

Tuskegee

Wherefore this busy labor without rest?
Is it an idle dream to which we cling,
Here where a thousand dusky toilers sing
Unto the world their hope? "Build we our best.
By hand and thought," they cry, "although unblessed."
So the great engines throb, and anvils ring,
And so the thought is wedded to the thing;
But what shall be the end, and what the test?
Dear God, we dare not answer, we can see
Not many steps ahead, but this we know—
If all our toilsome building is in vain,
Availing not to set our manhood free,
If envious hate roots out the seed we sow,
The South will wear eternally a stain.

LESLIE PINCKNEY HILL

CHRISTMAS AT MELROSE

Come home with me a little space
And browse about our ancient place,
Lay by your wonted troubles here
And have a turn of Christmas cheer.
These sober walls of weathered stone
Can tell a romance of their own,
And these wide rooms of devious line
Are kindly meant in their design.
Sometimes the north wind searches through,
But he shall not be rude to you.
We'll light a log of generous girth
For winter comfort, and the mirth
Of healthy children you shall see
About a sparkling Christmas tree.
Eleanor, leader of the fold,
Hermione with heart of gold,
Elaine with comprehending eyes,
And two more yet of coddling size,
Natalie pondering all that's said,
And Mary with the cherub head—
All these shall give you sweet content
And care-destroying merriment,
While one with true madonna grace
Moves round the glowing fire-place
Where father loves to muse aside
And grandma sits in silent pride.
And you may chafe the wasting oak,
Or freely pass the kindly joke
To mix with nuts and home-made cake
And apples set on coals to bake.
Or some fine carol we will sing
In honor of the Manger-King,
Or hear great Milton's organ verse
Or Plato's dialogue rehearse
What Socrates with his last breath
Sublimely said of life and death.

These dear delights we fain would share
With friend and kinsman everywhere,
And from our door see them depart
Each with a little lighter heart.

SUMMER MAGIC

So many cares to vex the day,
  So many fears to haunt the night,
My heart was all but weaned away
  From every lure of old delight.
Then summer came, announced by June,
  With beauty, miracle and mirth.
She hung aloft the rounding moon,
  She poured her sunshine on the earth,
She drove the sap and broke the bud,
  She set the crimson rose afire.
She stirred again my sullen blood,
  And waked in me a new desire.
Before my cottage door she spread
  The softest carpet nature weaves,
And deftly arched above my head
  A canopy of shady leaves.
Her nights were dreams of jeweled skies,
  Her days were bowers rife with song,
And many a scheme did she devise
  To heal the hurt and soothe the wrong.
For on the hill or in the dell,
  Or where the brook went leaping by
Or where the fields would surge and swell
  With golden wheat or bearded rye,
I felt her heart against my own,
  I breathed the sweetness of her breath,
Till all the cark of time had flown,
  And I was lord of life and death.

LESLIE PINCKNEY HILL

The Teacher

Lord, who am I to teach the way
To little children day by day,
So prone myself to go astray?

I teach them KNOWLEDGE, but I know
How faint they flicker and how low
The candles of my knowledge glow.

I teach them POWER to will and do,
But only now to learn anew
My own great weakness through and through.

I teach them LOVE for all mankind
And all God's creatures, but I find
My love comes lagging far behind.

Lord, if their guide I still must be,
Oh let the little children see
The teacher leaning hard on Thee.

LESLIE PINCKNEY HILL

EDWARD SMYTH JONES

A Song of Thanks

For the sun that shone at the dawn of spring,
For the flowers which bloom and the birds that sing,
For the verdant robe of the gray old earth,
For her coffers filled with their countless worth,
For the flocks which feed on a thousand hills,
For the rippling streams which turn the mills,
For the lowing herds in the lovely vale,
For the songs of gladness on the gale,—
From the Gulf and the Lakes to the Oceans' banks,—
Lord God of Hosts, we give Thee thanks!

For the farmer reaping his whitened fields,
For the bounty which the rich soil yields,
For the cooling dews and refreshing rains,
For the sun which ripens the golden grains,
For the bearded wheat and the fattened swine,
For the stallèd ox and the fruitful vine,
For the tubers large and cotton white,
For the kid and the lambkin frisk and blithe,
For the swan which floats near the river-banks,—
Lord God of Hosts, we give Thee thanks!

For the pumpkin sweet and the yellow yam,
For the corn and beans and the sugared ham,
For the plum and the peach and the apple red,
For the dear old press where the wine is tread,
For the cock which crows at the breaking dawn,
And the proud old "turk" of the farmer's barn,
For the fish which swim in the babbling brooks,
For the game which hide in the shady nooks,—
From the Gulf and the Lakes to the Oceans' banks—
Lord God of Hosts, we give Thee thanks!

For the sturdy oaks and the stately pines,
For the lead and the coal from the deep, dark mines,
For the silver ores of a thousand fold,

For the diamond bright and the yellow gold,
For the river boat and the flying train,
For the fleecy sail of the rolling main,
For the velvet sponge and the glossy pearl,
For the flag of peace which we now unfurl,—
From the Gulf and the Lakes to the Oceans' banks,—
Lord God of Hosts, we give Thee thanks!

For the lowly cot and the mansion fair,
For the peace and plenty together share,
For the Hand which guides us from above,
For Thy tender mercies, abiding love,
For the blessed home with its children gay,
For returnings of Thanksgiving Day,
For the bearing toils and the sharing cares,
We lift up our hearts in our songs and our prayers,—
From the Gulf and the Lakes to the Oceans' banks,—
Lord God of Hosts, we give Thee thanks!

EDWARD SMYTH JONES

RAY G. DANDRIDGE

Time to Die

Black brother, think you life so sweet
That you would live at any price?
Does mere existence balance with
The weight of your great sacrifice?
Or can it be you fear the grave
Enough to live and die a slave?
O Brother! be it better said,
When you are gone and tears are shed,
That your death was the stepping stone
Your children's children cross'd upon.
Men have died that men might live:
Look every foeman in the eye!
If necessary, your life give
For something, ere in vain you die.

'ITTLE TOUZLE HEAD

(To R. V.P.)

Cum, listen w'ile yore Unkel sings
Erbout how low sweet chariot swings,
Truint Angel, wifout wings,
Mah 'ittle Touzle Head.

Stop! Stop! How dare you laff et me,
Bekaze I foul de time an' key,
Thinks you dat I is Black Pattie,
Mah 'ittle Touzle Head?

O, Honey Lam'! dem sparklin' eyes,
Dat offen laffs an' selem cries,
Is sho a God gib natchel prize,
Mah 'ittle Touzle Head.

An' doze wee ban's so sof an' sweet,
Mates wid dem toddlin', velvet feet,
Jes to roun' you out, complete,
Mah 'ittle Touzle Head.

Sma't! youse sma't ez sma't kin be,
Knows yore evah A, B, C,
Plum on down to X, Y, Z,
Mah 'ittle Touzle Head.

De man doan know how much he miss,
Ef he ain't got no niece lak dis;
Fro yore Unkel one mo' kiss,
Mah 'ittle Touzle Head!

I wist sum magic w'u'd ellow,
(By charm or craf'—doan mattah how)
You stay jes lak you is right now,
Mah 'ittle Touzle Head.

RAY G. DANDRIDGE

Zalka Peetruza

(Who Was Christened Lucy Jane)

She danced, near nude, to tom-tom beat,
With swaying arms and flying feet,
'Mid swirling spangles, gauze and lace,
Her all was dancing—save her face.

A conscience, dumb to brooding fears,
Companioned hearing deaf to cheers;
A body, marshalled by the will,
Kept dancing while a heart stood still:

And eyes obsessed with vacant stare,
Looked over heads to empty air,
As though they sought to find therein
Redemption for a maiden sin.

'Twas thus, amid force driven grace,
We found the lost look on her face;
And then, to us, did it occur
That, though we saw—we saw not her.

Sprin' Fevah

Dar's a lazy, sortah hazy
Feelin' grips me, thoo an' thoo;
An' I feels lak doin' less dan enythin';
Dough de saw is sharp an' greasy,
Dough de task et han' is easy,
An' de day am fair an' breezy,
Dar's a thief dat steals embition in de win'.

Kaint defy it, kaint deny it,
Kaze it jes won't be denied;
Its a mos' pursistin' stubbern sortah thin';
Anti Tox' doan neutrolize it;
Doctahs fail to analyze it;
So I yiel's (dough I despise it)
To dat res'less, wretchit fevah evah Sprin'.

RAY G. DANDRIDGE

De Drum Majah

He's struttin' sho ernuff,
Wearin' a lady's muff
En' ways erpon his head,
Red coat ob reddest red,
Purtty white satin ves',
Gole braid ercross de ches';
Goo'ness! he cuts a stunt,
Prancin' out dar in frunt,
 Leadin' his ban'.

Wen dat ah whistle blows,
Each man behine him knows
'Zacklee whut he mus' do;
You bet! he dues it, too.
W'en dat brass stick he twirls,
Ole maids an' lub-sick gurls
Looks on wid longin' eyes,
Dey simply idolize
 Dat han'sum man.

Sweet fife an' piccalo,
Bofe warblin' sof an' lo'
Slide ho'n an' saxophones,
Jazz syncopated tones,
Snare drum an' lead cornet,
Alto an' clarinet,
Las', but not least, dar cum
Cymbals an' big bass drum—
 O! whut a ban'!

Cose, we all undahstan'
Each piece he'ps maik de ban',
But dey all mus' be led,
Sum one mus' be de head:
No doubt, de centipede

Has all de laigs he need,
But take erway de head,
Po' centipede am dead;
     So am de ban'.

FENTON JOHNSON

CHILDREN OF THE SUN

We are children of the sun,
    Rising sun!
Weaving Southern destiny,
Waiting for the mighty hour
When our Shiloh shall appear
With the flaming sword of right,
With the steel of brotherhood,
And emboss in crimson die
Liberty! Fraternity!

We are the star-dust folk,
    Striving folk!
Sorrow songs have lulled to rest;
Seething passions wrought through wrongs,
Led us where the moon rays dip
In the night of dull despair,
Showed us where the star gleams shine,
And the mystic symbols glow—
Liberty! Fraternity!

We have come through cloud and mist,
    Mighty men!
Dusk has kissed our sleep-born eyes,
Reared for us a mystic throne
In the splendor of the skies,
That shall always be for us,
Children of the Nazarene,
Children who shall ever sing
Liberty! Fraternity!

THE NEW DAY

From a vision red with war I awoke and saw the Prince
    of Peace hovering over No Man's Land.
Loud the whistles blew and the thunder of cannon was
    drowned by the happy shouting of the people.
From the Sinai that faces Armageddon I heard this chant
    from the throats of white-robed angels:

    Blow your trumpets, little children!
    From the East and from the West,
    From the cities in the valley,
    From God's dwelling on the mountain,
    Blow your blast that Peace might know
    She is Queen of God's great army.
    With the crying blood of millions
    We have written deep her name
    In the Book of all the Ages;
    With the lilies in the valley,
    With the roses by the Mersey,
    With the golden flower of Jersey
    We have crowned her smooth young temples.
    Where her footsteps cease to falter
    Golden grain will greet the morning,
    Where her chariot descends
    Shall be broken down the altars
    Of the gods of dark disturbance.
    Nevermore shall men know suffering,
    Nevermore shall women wailing
    Shake to grief the God of Heaven.
    From the East and from the West,
    From the cities in the valley,
    From God's dwelling on the mountain,
    Little children, blow your trumpets!

From Ethiopia, groaning 'neath her heavy burdens, I
    heard the music of the old slave songs.
I heard the wail of warriors, dusk brown, who grimly

            FENTON JOHNSON

fought the fight of others in the trenches of Mars.
I heard the plea of blood-stained men of dusk and the
crimson in my veins leapt furiously.

Forget not, O my brothers, how we fought
In No Man's Land that peace might come again!
Forget not, O my brothers, how we gave
Red blood to save the freedom of the world!
We were not free, our tawny hands were tied;
But Belgium's plight and Serbia's woes we shared
Each rise of sun or setting of the moon.
So when the bugle blast had called us forth
We went not like the surly brute of yore
But, as the Spartan, proud to give the world
The freedom that we never knew nor shared.
These chains, O brothers mine, have weighed us down
As Samson in the temple of the gods;
Unloosen them and let us breathe the air
That makes the goldenrod the flower of Christ.
For we have been with thee in No Man's Land,
Through lake of fire and down to Hell itself;
And now we ask of thee our liberty,
Our freedom in the land of Stars and Stripes.

I am glad that the Prince of Peace is hovering over No Man's Land.

Tired

I am tired of work; I am tired of building up somebody else's
    civilization.

Let us take a rest, M'Lissy Jane.

I will go down to the Last Chance Saloon, drink a gallon or two of
    gin, shoot a game or two of dice and sleep the rest of the night on
    one of Mike's barrels.

You will let the old shanty go to rot, the white people's clothes turn to
    dust, and the Calvary Baptist Church sink to the bottomless pit.

You will spend your days forgetting you married me and your nights
    hunting the warm gin Mike serves the ladies in the rear of the Last
    Chance Saloon.

Throw the children into the river; civilization has given us too many.
    It is better to die than it is to grow up and find out that you are
    colored.

Pluck the stars out of the heavens. The stars mark our destiny. The
    stars marked my destiny.

I am tired of civilization.

The Banjo Player

There is music in me, the music of a peasant people.
I wander through the levee, picking my banjo and singing
    my songs of the cabin and the field. At the
    Last Chance Saloon I am as welcome as the violets
    in March; there is always food and drink for me
    there, and the dimes of those who love honest music.
    Behind the railroad tracks the little children clap
    their hands and love me as they love Kris Kringle.

But I fear that I am a failure. Last night a woman called me a
    troubadour. What is a troubadour?

The Scarlet Woman

Once I was good like the Virgin Mary and the Minister's wife.

My father worked for Mr. Pullman and white people's tips; but he
died two days after his insurance expired.

I had nothing, so I had to go to work.

All the stock I had was a white girl's education and a face that
enchanted the men of both races.

Starvation danced with me.

So when Big Lizzie, who kept a house for white men, came to me
with tales of fortune that I could reap from the sale of my virtue I
bowed my head to Vice.

Now I can drink more gin than any man for miles around.

Gin is better than all the water in Lethe.

R. NATHANIEL DETT

THE RUBINSTEIN STACCATO ETUDE

Staccato! Staccato!
Leggier agitato!
    In and out does the melody twist—
Unique proposition
Is this composition.
    (Alas! for the player who hasn't the wrist!)
Now in the dominant
Theme ringing prominent,
    Bass still repeating its one monotone,
Double notes crying,
Up keyboard go flying,
    The change to the minor comes in like a groan.
Without a cessation
A chaste modulation
    Hastens adown to subdominant key,
Where melody mellow-like
Singing so 'cello-like
    Rises and falls in a wild ecstasy.
Scarce is this finished
When chords all diminished
    Break loose in a patter that comes down like rain,
A pedal-point wonder
Rivaling thunder.
    Now all is mad agitation again.
Like laughter jolly
Begins the finale;
    Again does the 'cello its tones seem to lend
Diminuendo ad molto crescendo.
    Ah! Rubinstein only could make such an end!

R. NATHANIEL DETT

GEORGIA DOUGLAS JOHNSON

The Heart of a Woman

The heart of a woman goes forth with the dawn,
As a lone bird, soft winging, so restlessly on,
Afar o'er life's turrets and vales does it roam
In the wake of those echoes the heart calls home.

The heart of a woman falls back with the night,
And enters some alien cage in its plight,
And tries to forget it has dreamed of the stars
While it breaks, breaks, breaks on the sheltering bars.

GEORGIA DOUGLAS JOHNSON

Youth

The dew is on the grasses, dear,
    The blush is on the rose,
And swift across our dial-youth,
    A shifting shadow goes.

The primrose moments, lush with bliss,
    Exhale and fade away,
Life may renew the Autumn time,
    But nevermore the May!

GEORGIA DOUGLAS JOHNSON

Lost Illusions

Oh, for the veils of my far away youth,
Shielding my heart from the blaze of the truth,
Why did I stray from their shelter and grow
Into the sadness that follows—to know!

Impotent atom with desolate gaze
Threading the tumult of hazardous ways—
Oh, for the veils, for the veils of my youth
Veils that hung low o'er the blaze of the truth!

I Want to Die While You Love Me

I want to die while you love me,
 While yet you hold me fair,
While laughter lies upon my lips
 And lights are in my hair.

I want to die while you love me,
 And bear to that still bed,
Your kisses turbulent, unspent
 To warm me when I'm dead.

I want to die while you love me
 Oh, who would care to live
Till love has nothing more to ask
 And nothing more to give!

I want to die while you love me
 And never, never see
The glory of this perfect day
 Grow dim or cease to be.

GEORGIA DOUGLAS JOHNSON

WELT

Would I might mend the fabric of my youth
That daily flaunts its tatters to my eyes,
Would I might compromise awhile with truth
Until our moon now waxing, wanes and dies.

For I would go a further while with you,
And drain this cup so tantalant and fair
Which meets my parched lips like cooling dew,
Ere time has brushed cold fingers thru my hair!

My Little Dreams

I'm folding up my little dreams
Within my heart to-night,
And praying I may soon forget
The torture of their sight.

For Time's deft fingers scroll my brow
With fell relentless art—
I'm folding up my little dreams
To-night, within my heart!

CLAUDE MCKAY

THE LYNCHING

His spirit in smoke ascended to high heaven.
His father, by the crudest way of pain,
Had bidden him to his bosom once again;
The awful sin remained still unforgiven.
All night a bright and solitary star
(Perchance the one that ever guided him,
Yet gave him up at last to Fate's wild whim)
Hung pitifully o'er the swinging char.
Day dawned, and soon the mixed crowds came to view
The ghastly body swaying in the sun:
The women thronged to look, but never a one
Showed sorrow in her eyes of steely blue;
And little lads, lynchers that were to be,
Danced round the dreadful thing in fiendish glee.

If We Must Die

If we must die—let it not be like hogs
Hunted and penned in an inglorious spot,
While round us bark the mad and hungry dogs,
Making their mock at our accursed lot.
If we must die—oh, let us nobly die,
So that our precious blood may not be shed
In vain; then even the monsters we defy
Shall be constrained to honor us though dead!

Oh, Kinsmen! We must meet the common foe;
Though far outnumbered, let us still be brave,
And for their thousand blows deal one death-blow!
What though before us lies the open grave?
Like men we'll face the murderous, cowardly pack,
Pressed to the wall, dying, but—fighting back!

CLAUDE MCKAY

To the White Fiends

Think you I am not fiend and savage too?
Think you I could not arm me with a gun
And shoot down ten of you for every one
Of my black brothers murdered, burnt by you?
Be not deceived, for every deed you do
I could match—out-match: am I not Africa's son,
Black of that black land where black deeds are done?

But the Almighty from the darkness drew
My soul and said: Even thou shalt be a light
Awhile to burn on the benighted earth,
Thy dusky face I set among the white
For thee to prove thyself of highest worth;
Before the world is swallowed up in night,
To show thy little lamp: go forth, go forth!

The Harlem Dancer

Applauding youths laughed with young prostitutes
And watched her perfect, half-clothed body sway;
Her voice was like the sound of blended flutes
Blown by black players upon a picnic day.
She sang and danced on gracefully and calm,
The light gauze hanging loose about her form;
To me she seemed a proudly-swaying palm
Grown lovelier for passing through a storm.
Upon her swarthy neck black, shiny curls
Profusely fell; and, tossing coins in praise,
The wine-flushed, bold-eyed boys, and even the girls,
Devoured her with their eager, passionate gaze;
But, looking at her falsely-smiling face
I knew her self was not in that strange place.

CLAUDE MCKAY

Harlem Shadows

I hear the halting footsteps of a lass
    In Negro Harlem when the night lets fall
Its veil. I see the shapes of girls who pass
    Eager to heed desire's insistent call:
Ah, little dark girls, who in slippered feet
    Go prowling through the night from street to street.

Through the long night until the silver break
    Of day the little gray feet know no rest,
Through the lone night until the last snow-flake
    Has dropped from heaven upon the earth's white breast,
The dusky, half-clad girls of tired feet
    Are trudging, thinly shod, from street to street.

Ah, stern harsh world, that in the wretched way
    Of poverty, dishonor and disgrace,
Has pushed the timid little feet of clay.
    The sacred brown feet of my fallen race!
Ah, heart of me, the weary, weary feet
    In Harlem wandering from street to street.

After the Winter

Some day, when trees have shed their leaves,
    And against the morning's white
The shivering birds beneath the eaves
    Have sheltered for the night,
We'll turn our faces southward, love,
    Toward the summer isle
Where bamboos spire the shafted grove
    And wide-mouthed orchids smile.

And we will seek the quiet hill
    Where towers the cotton tree,
And leaps the laughing crystal rill,
    And works the droning bee.
And we will build a lonely nest
    Beside an open glade,
And there forever will we rest,
    O love—O nut-brown maid!

CLAUDE MCKAY

Spring in New Hampshire

Too green the springing April grass,
Too blue the silver speckled sky,
For me to linger here, alas,
While happy winds go laughing by,
Wasting the golden hours indoors,
Washing windows and scrubbing floors.

Too wonderful the April night,
Too faintly sweet the first May flowers,
The stars too gloriously bright,
For me to spend the evening hours,
When fields are fresh and streams are leaping,
Wearied, exhausted, dully sleeping.

The Tired Worker

O whisper, O my soul!—the afternoon
Is waning into evening—whisper soft!
Peace, O my rebel heart! for soon the moon
From out its misty veil will swing aloft!
Be patient, weary body, soon the night
Will wrap thee gently in her sable sheet,
And with a leaden sigh thou wilt invite
To rest thy tired hands and aching feet.
The wretched day was theirs, the night is mine;
Come, tender sleep, and fold me to thy breast.
But what steals out the gray clouds red like wine?
O dawn! O dreaded dawn! O let me rest!
Weary my veins, my brain, my life,—have pity!
No! Once again the hard, the ugly city.

CLAUDE MCKAY

The Barrier

I must not gaze at them although
    Your eyes are dawning day;
I must not watch you as you go
    Your sun-illumined way;

I hear but I must never heed
    The fascinating note,
Which, fluting like a river-reed,
    Comes from your trembling throat;

I must not see upon your face
    Love's softly glowing spark;
For there's the barrier of race,
    You're fair and I am dark.

To O. E. A.

Your voice is the color of a robin's breast,
    And there's a sweet sob in it like rain—still rain in the night.
Among the leaves of the trumpet-tree, close to his nest,
    The pea-dove sings, and each note thrills me with strange delight
Like the words, wet with music, that well from your trembling throat.
      I'm afraid of your eyes, they're so bold,
        Searching me through, reading my thoughts, shining like gold.
But sometimes they are gentle and soft like the dew on the lips of the
    eucharis
Before the sun comes warm with his lover's kiss,
    You are sea-foam, pure with the star's loveliness,
Not mortal, a flower, a fairy, too fair for the beauty-shorn earth,
All wonderful things, all beautiful things, gave of their wealth to your
    birth:
    O I love you so much, not recking of passion, that I feel it is wrong,
      But men will love you, flower, fairy, non-mortal spirit burdened
    with flesh,
Forever, life-long.

FLAME-HEART

So much have I forgotten in ten years,
    So much in ten brief years; I have forgot
What time the purple apples come to juice
    And what month brings the shy forget-me-not;
Forgotten is the special, startling season
    Of some beloved tree's flowering and fruiting,
What time of year the ground doves brown the fields
    And fill the noonday with their curious fluting:
I have forgotten much, but still remember
The poinsettia's red, blood-red in warm December.

I still recall the honey-fever grass,
    But I cannot bring back to mind just when
We rooted them out of the ping-wing path
    To stop the mad bees in the rabbit pen.
I often try to think in what sweet month
    The languid painted ladies used to dapple
The yellow bye road mazing from the main,
    Sweet with the golden threads of the rose-apple:
I have forgotten, strange, but quite remember
The poinsettia's red, blood-red in warm December.

What weeks, what months, what time o' the mild year
    We cheated school to have our fling at tops?
What days our wine-thrilled bodies pulsed with joy
    Feasting upon blackberries in the copse?
Oh, some I know! I have embalmed the days,
    Even the sacred moments, when we played,
All innocent of passion uncorrupt,
    At noon and evening in the flame-heart's shade:
We were so happy, happy,—I remember
Beneath the poinsettia's red in warm December.

Two-an'-Six

Merry voices chatterin',
Nimble feet dem patterin',
Big an' little, faces gay,
Happy day dis market day.

Sateday, de marnin' break,
Soon, soon market-people wake;
An' de light shine from de moon
While dem boy, wid pantaloon
Roll up ober dem knee-pan,
'Tep across de buccra lan'
To de pastur whe' de harse
Feed along wid de jackass,
An' de mule cant' in de track
Wid him tail up in him back,
All de ketchin' to defy,
No ca' how dem boy might try.

In de early marnin'-tide,
When de cocks crow on de hill
An' de stars are shinin' still,
Mirrie by de fireside
Hots de coffee for de lads
Comin' ridin' on de pads
T'rown across dem animul—
Donkey, harse too, an' de mule,
Which at last had come do'n cool.
On de bit dem hol' dem full:
Racin' ober pastur' lan',
See dem comin' ebery man,
Comin' fe de steamin' tea
Ober hilly track an' lea.

Hard-wuk'd donkey on de road
Trottin' wid him ushal load,
Hamper pack' wi' yam an' grain,

Sour-sop, and Gub'nor cane.
Cous' Sun sits in hired dray,
Drivin' 'long de market way;
Whole week grindin' sugar cane
T'rough de boilin' sun an' rain,
Now, a'ter de toilin' hard,
He goes seekin' his reward,
While he's thinkin' in him min'
Of de dear ones lef behin',
Of de loved though ailin' wife,
Darlin' treasure of his life,
An' de picknies, six in all,
Whose 'nuff burdens 'pon him fall:
Seben lovin' ones in need,
Seben hungry mouths fe feed;
On deir wants he thinks alone,
Neber dreamin' of his own,
But gwin' on wid joyful face
Till him re'ch de market-place.

Sugar bears no price to-day,
Though it is de mont' o' May,
When de time is hellish hot,
An' de water cocoanut
An' de cane bebridge is nice,
Mix' up wid a lilly ice.
Big an' little, great an' small,
Afou yam is all de call;
Sugar tup an' gill a quart,
Yet de people hab de heart
Wantin' brater top o' i',
Want de sweatin' higgler fe
Ram de pan an' pile i' up,
Yet sell i' fe so-so tup.

Cousin Sun is lookin' sad,
As de market is so bad;
'Pon him han' him res' him chin,
Quietly sit do'n thinkin'

Of de loved wife sick in bed,
An' de children to be fed—
What de laborers would say
When dem know him couldn' pay;
Also what about de mill
Whe' him hire from ole Bill;
So him think, an' think on so,
Till him t'oughts no more could go.

Then he got up an' began
Pickin' up him sugar-pan:
In his ears rang t'rough de din
"Only two-an'-six a tin'."
What a tale he'd got to tell,
How bad, bad de sugar sell!
Tekin' out de lee amount,
Him set do'n an' begin count
All de time him min' deh doubt
How expenses would pay out;
Ah, it gnawed him like de ticks,
Sugar sell fe two-an'-six!

So he journeys on de way,
Feelinl sad dis market day;
No e'en buy a little cake
To gi'e baby when she wake,—
Passin' 'long de candy-shop
'Douten eben mek a stop
To buy drops fe las'y son,
For de lilly cash nea' done.
So him re'ch him own a groun',
An' de children scamper roun',
Each one stretchin' out him han',
Lookin' to de poor sad man.

Oh, how much he felt de blow,
As he watched dem face fall low,
When dem wait an' nuttin' came
An' drew back deir han's wid shame!

But de sick wife kissed his brow:
"Sun, don't get down-hearted now;
Ef we only pay expense
We mus' wuk we common-sense,
Cut an' carve, an' carve an' cut,
Mek gill sarbe fe quattiewut;
We mus' try mek two ends meet
Neber mind how hard be it.
We won't mind de haul an' pull,
While dem pickny belly full."

An' de shadow lef' him face,
An' him felt an inward peace,
As he blessed his better part
For her sweet an' gentle heart:
"Dear one o' my heart, my breat',
Won't I lub you to de deat'?
When my heart is weak an' sad,
Who but you can mek it glad?"

So dey kissed an' kissed again,
An' deir t'oughts were not on pain,
But was 'way down in de sout'
Where dey'd wedded in deir yout',
In de marnin' of deir life
Free from all de grief an' strife,
Happy in de marnin' light,
Never thinkin' of de night.

So dey k'lated eberyt'ing;
An' de profit it could bring,
A'ter all de business fix',
Was a princely two-an'-six.

JOSEPH S. COTTER, JR.

A Prayer

As I lie in bed,
Flat on my back;
There passes across my ceiling
An endless panorama of things—
Quick steps of gay-voiced children,
Adolescence in its wondering silences,
Maid and man on moonlit summer's eve,
Women in the holy glow of Motherhood,
Old men gazing silently thru the twilight
Into the beyond.
O God, give me words to make my dream-children live.

And What Shall You Say?

Brother, come!
And let us go unto our God.
And when we stand before Him
I shall say—
"Lord, I do not hate,
I am hated.
I scourge no one,
I am scourged.
I covet no lands,
My lands are coveted.
I mock no peoples,
My people are mocked."
And, brother, what shall you say?

JOSEPH S. COTTER, JR.

Is It Because I am Black?

Why do men smile when I speak,
And call my speech
The whimperings of a babe
That cries but knows not what it wants?
Is it because I am black?

Why do men sneer when I arise
And stand in their councils,
And look them eye to eye,
And speak their tongue?
Is it because I am black?

JOSEPH S. COTTER, JR.

The Band of Gideon

The band of Gideon roam the sky,
The howling wind is their war-cry,
The thunder's roll is their trump's peal,
And the lightning's flash their vengeful steel.
  Each black cloud
  Is a fiery steed.
  And they cry aloud
  With each strong deed,
"The sword of the Lord and Gideon."

And men below rear temples high
And mock their God with reasons why,
And live in arrogance, sin and shame,
And rape their souls for the world's good name.
  Each black cloud
  Is a fiery steed.
  And they cry aloud
  With each strong deed,
"The sword of the Lord and Gideon."

The band of Gideon roam the sky
And view the earth with baleful eye;
In holy wrath they scourge the land
With earth-quake, storm and burning brand.
  Each black cloud
  Is a fiery steed.
  And they cry aloud
  With each strong deed,
"The sword of the Lord and Gideon."

The lightnings flash and the thunders roll,
And "Lord have mercy on my soul,"
Cry men as they fall on the stricken sod,
In agony searching for their God.
  Each black cloud
  Is a fiery steed.

    JOSEPH S. COTTER, JR.

And they cry aloud
With each strong deed,
"The sword of the Lord and Gideon."

And men repent and then forget
That heavenly wrath they ever met,
The band of Gideon yet will come
And strike their tongues of blasphemy dumb.
Each black cloud
Is a fiery steed.
And they cry aloud
With each strong deed,
"The sword of the Lord and Gideon."

Rain Music

On the dusty earth-drum
    Beats the falling rain;
Now a whispered murmur,
    Now a louder strain.

Slender, silvery drumsticks,
    On an ancient drum,
Beat the mellow music
    Bidding life to come.
Chords of earth awakened,
    Notes of greening spring,
Rise and fall triumphant
    Over every thing.

Slender, silvery drumsticks
    Beat the long tattoo—
God, the Great Musician,
    Calling life anew.

JOSEPH S. COTTER, JR.

Supplication

I am so tired and weary,
  So tired of the endless fight,
So weary of waiting the dawn
  And finding endless night.

That I ask but rest and quiet—
  Rest for days that are gone,
And quiet for the little space
  That I must journey on.

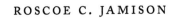

ROSCOE C. JAMISON

The Negro Soldiers

These truly are the Brave,
These men who cast aside
Old memories, to walk the blood-stained pave
Of Sacrifice, joining the solemn tide
That moves away, to suffer and to die
For Freedom—when their own is yet denied!
O Pride! O Prejudice! When they pass by,
Hail them, the Brave, for you now crucified!

These truly are the Free,
These souls that grandly rise
Above base dreams of vengeance for their wrongs,
Who march to war with visions in their eyes
Of Peace through Brotherhood, lifting glad songs,
Aforetime, while they front the firing line.
Stand and behold! They take the field to-day,
Shedding their blood like Him now held divine,
That those who mock might find a better way!

ROSCOE C. JAMISON

JESSIE FAUSET

La Vie C'est la Vie

On summer afternoons I sit
Quiescent by you in the park,
And idly watch the sunbeams gild
And tint the ash-trees' bark.

Or else I watch the squirrels frisk
And chaffer in the grassy lane;
And all the while I mark your voice
Breaking with love and pain.

I know a woman who would give
Her chance of heaven to take my place;
To see the love-light in your eyes,
The love-glow on your face!

And there's a man whose lightest word
Can set my chilly blood afire;
Fulfilment of his least behest
Defines my life's desire.

But he will none of me, Nor I
Of you. Nor you of her. 'Tis said
The world is full of jests like these.—
I wish that I were dead.

CHRISTMAS EVE IN FRANCE

Oh little Christ, why do you sigh
    As you look down to-night
On breathless France, on bleeding France,
    And all her dreadful plight?
What bows your childish head so low?
    What turns your cheek so white?

Oh little Christ, why do you moan,
    What is it that you see
In mourning France, in martyred France,
    And her great agony?
Does she recall your own dark day,
    Your own Gethsemane?

Oh little Christ, why do you weep,
    Why flow your tears so sore
For pleading France, for praying France,
    A suppliant at God's door?
"God sweetened not my cup," you say,
    "Shall He for France do more?"

Oh little Christ, what can this mean,
    Why must this horror be
For fainting France, for faithful France,
    And her sweet chivalry?
"I bled to free all men," you say
    "France bleeds to keep men free."

Oh little, lovely Christ—you smile!
    What guerdon is in store
For gallant France, for glorious France,
    And all her valiant corps?
"Behold I live, and France, like me,
    Shall live for evermore."

JESSIE FAUSET

Dead Fires

If this is peace, this dead and leaden thing,
    Then better far the hateful fret, the sting.
Better the wound forever seeking balm
    Than this gray calm!

Is this pain's surcease? Better far the ache,
    The long-drawn dreary day, the night's white wake,
Better the choking sigh, the sobbing breath
    Than passion's death!

ORIFLAMME

"I can remember when I was a little, young girl, how my old mammy would sit out of doors in the evenings and look up at the stars and groan, and I would say, 'Mammy, what makes you groan so?' And she would say, 'I am groaning to think of my poor children; they do not know where I be and I don't know where they be. I look up at the stars and they look up at the stars!'"

—*Sojourner Truth*

I think I see her sitting bowed and black,
    Stricken and seared with slavery's mortal scars,
Reft of her children, lonely, anguished, yet
    Still looking at the stars.

Symbolic mother, we thy myriad sons,
    Pounding our stubborn hearts on Freedom's bars,
Clutching our birthright, fight with faces set,
    Still visioning the stars!

JESSIE FAUSET

Oblivion

From the French of Massillon Coicou (Haiti)

I hope when I am dead that I shall lie
    In some deserted grave—I cannot tell you why,
But I should like to sleep in some neglected spot
    Unknown to every one, by every one forgot.

There lying I should taste with my dead breath
    The utter lack of life, the fullest sense of death;
And I should never hear the note of jealousy or hate,
    The tribute paid by passersby to tombs of state.

To me would never penetrate the prayers and tears
    That futilely bring torture to dead and dying ears;
There I should lie annihilate and my dead heart would bless
    Oblivion—the shroud and envelope of happiness.

ANNE SPENCER

Before the Feast of Shushan

Garden of Shushan!
After Eden, all terrace, pool, and flower recollect thee:
Ye weavers in saffron and haze and Tyrian purple,
Tell yet what range in color wakes the eye;
Sorcerer, release the dreams born here when
Drowsy, shifting palm-shade enspells the brain;
And sound! ye with harp and flute ne'er essay
Before these star-noted birds escaped from paradise awhile to
Stir all dark, and dear, and passionate desire, till mine
Arms go out to be mocked by the softly kissing body of the wind—
Slave, send Vashti to her King!

The fiery wattles of the sun startle into flame
The marbled towers of Shushan:
So at each day's wane, two peers—the one in
Heaven, the other on earth—welcome with their
Splendor the peerless beauty of the Queen.

Cushioned at the Queen's feet and upon her knee
Finding glory for mine head,—still, nearly shamed
Am I, the King, to bend and kiss with sharp
Breath the olive-pink of sandaled toes between;
Or lift me high to the magnet of a gaze, dusky,
Like the pool when but the moon-ray strikes to its depth;
Or closer press to crush a grape 'gainst lips redder
Than the grape, a rose in the night of her hair;
Then—Sharon's Rose in my arms.

And I am hard to force the petals wide;
And you are fast to suffer and be sad.
Is any prophet come to teach a new thing
Now in a more apt time?
Have him 'maze how you say love is sacrament;
How says Vashti, love is both bread and wine;
How to the altar may not come to break and drink,
Hulky flesh nor fleshly spirit!

I, thy lord, like not manna for meat as a Judahn;
I, thy master, drink, and red wine, plenty, and when
I thirst. Eat meat, and full, when I hunger.
I, thy King, teach you and leave you, when I list.
No woman in all Persia sets out strange action
To confuse Persia's lord—
Love is but desire and thy purpose fulfillment;
I, thy King, so say!

At the Carnival

Gay little Girl-of-the-Diving-Tank,
I desire a name for you,
Nice, as a right glove fits;
For you—who amid the malodorous
Mechanics of this unlovely thing,
Are darling of spirit and form.
I know you—a glance, and what you are
Sits-by-the-fire in my heart.
My Limousine-Lady knows you, or
Why does the slant-envy of her eye mark
Your straight air and radiant inclusive smile?
Guilt pins a fig-leaf; Innocence is its own adorning.
The bull-necked man knows you—this first time
His itching flesh sees form divine and vibrant health
And thinks not of his avocation.
I came incuriously—
Set on no diversion save that my mind
Might safely nurse its brood of misdeeds
In the presence of a blind crowd.
The color of life was gray.
Everywhere the setting seemed right
For my mood.
Here the sausage and garlic booth
Sent unholy incense skyward;
There a quivering female-thing
Gestured assignations, and lied
To call it dancing;
There, too, were games of chance
With chances for none;
But oh! Girl-of-the-Tank, at last!
Gleaming Girl, how intimately pure and free
The gaze you send the crowd,
As though you know the dearth of beauty
In its sordid life.
We need you—my Limousine-Lady,
The bull-necked man and I.

ANNE SPENCER

Seeing you here brave and water-clean,
Leaven for the heavy ones of earth,
I am swift to feel that what makes
The plodder glad is good; and
Whatever is good is God.
The wonder is that you are here;
I have seen the queer in queer places,
But never before a heaven-fed
Naiad of the Carnival-Tank!
Little Diver, Destiny for you,
Like as for me, is shod in silence;
Years may seep into your soul
The bacilli of the usual and the expedient;
I implore Neptune to claim his child to-day!

The Wife-Woman

Maker-of-Sevens in the scheme of things
From earth to star;
Thy cycle holds whatever is fate, and
Over the border the bar.
Though rank and fierce the mariner
Sailing the seven seas,
He prays, as he holds his glass to his eyes,
Coaxing the Pleiades.

I cannot love them; and I feel your glad
Chiding from the grave,
That my all was only worth at all, what
Joy to you it gave.
These seven links the *Law* compelled
For the human chain—
I cannot love *them*; and *you*, oh,
Seven-fold months in Flanders slain!

A jungle there, a cave here, bred six
And a million years,
Sure and strong, mate for mate, such
Love as culture fears;
I gave you clear the oil and wine;
You saved me your hob and hearth—
See how *even* life may be ere the
Sickle comes and leaves a swath.

But I can wait the seven of moons,
Or years I spare,
Hoarding the heart's plenty, nor spend
A drop, nor share—
So long but outlives a smile and
A silken gown;
Then gaily I reach up from my shroud,
And you, glory-clad, reach down.

TRANSLATION

We trekked into a far country,
My friend and I.
Our deeper content was never spoken,
But each knew all the other said.
He told me how calm his soul was laid
By the lack of anvil and strife.
"The wooing kestrel," I said, "mutes his mating-note
To please the harmony of this sweet silence."
And when at the day's end
We laid tired bodies 'gainst
The loose warm sands,
And the air fleeced its particles for a coverlet;
When star after star came out
To guard their lovers in oblivion—
My soul so leapt that my evening prayer
Stole my morning song!

DUNBAR

Ah, how poets sing and die!
Make one song and Heaven takes it;
Have one heart and Beauty breaks it;
Chatterton, Shelley, Keats and I—
Ah, how poets sing and die!

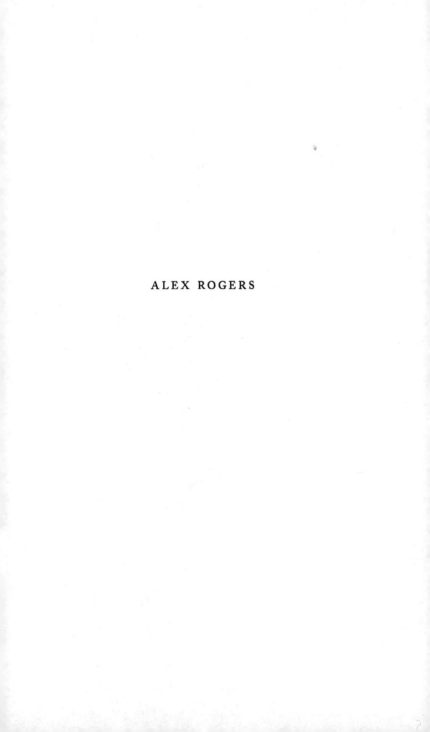

ALEX ROGERS

Why Adam Sinned

"I heeard da ole folks talkin' in our house da other night
'Bout Adam in da scripchuh long ago.
Da lady folks all 'bused him, sed, he knowed it wus'n right
An' 'cose da men folks dey all sed, "Dat's so."
I felt sorry fuh Mistuh Adam, an' I felt like puttin' in,
'Cause I knows mo' dan dey do, all 'bout whut made Adam sin:

Adam nevuh had no Mammy, fuh to take him on her knee
An' teach him right fum wrong an' show him
Things he ought to see.
I knows down in my heart—he'd-a let dat apple be
But Adam nevuh had no dear old Ma-am-my.

He nevuh knowed no chilehood roun' da ole log cabin do',
He nevuh knowed no pickaninny life.
He started in a great big grown up man, an' whut is mo',
He nevuh had da right kind uf a wife.
Jes s'pose he'd had a Mammy when dat temptin' did begin
An' she'd a come an' tole him
"Son, don' eat dat—dat's a sin."

But, Adam nevuh had no Mammy fuh to take him on her knee
An' teach him right fum wrong an' show him
Things he ought to see.
I knows down in my heart he'd a let dat apple be,
But Adam nevuh had no dear old Ma-am-my.

ALEX ROGERS

The Rain Song

BRO. SIMMONS: "Walk right in Brother Wilson—how you feelin'
today?"

BRO. WILSON: "Jes Mod'rate, Brother Simmons, but den I ginnerly
feels dat way."

BRO. SIMMONS: "Here's White an' Black an' Brown an' Green; how's
all you gent'men's been?",

BRO. WHITE: "My health is good but my bus'ness slack."

BRO. BLACK: "I'se been suff'rin' lots wid pains in my back."

BRO. BROWN: "My ole 'ooman's sick, but I'se alright—"

BRO. GREEN: "Yes, I went aftuh Doctuh fuh her 'tuther
night—"

BRO. SIMMONS: "Here's Sandy Turner, as I live!"

BRO. TURNER: "Yes, I didn' 'spect to git here—but here I is!"

BRO. SIMMONS: "Now, gent'mens, make yo'selves to home,
Dare's nothin' to fear—my ole 'ooman's gone—
My stars; da weather's pow'ful warm—
I wouldn' be s'prised ef we had a storm."

BRO. BROWN: "No, Brother Simmons, we kin safely say—
'Tain't gwine to be no storm to-day
Kase here am facts dat's mighty plain
An' any time you sees 'em you kin look fuh rain:
Any time you hears da cheers an' tables crack
An' da folks wid rheumatics—dare jints is on da rack—"

ALL: "Lookout fuh rain, rain, rain.
"When da ducks quack loud an' da peacocks cry,
An' da far off hills seems to be right nigh,
Prepare fuh rain, rain, rain!

"When da ole cat on da hearth wid her velvet paws
'Gins to wipin' over her whiskered jaws,
Sho' sign o' rain, rain, rain!

"When da frog's done changed his yaller vest,
An' in his brown suit he is dressed,
Mo' rain, an' still mo' rain!

"When you notice da air it Stan's stock still,
  An' da blackbird's voice it gits so awful shrill,
  Dat am da time fuh rain.

"When yo' dog quits bones an' begins to fas',
  An' when you see him eatin'; he's eatin' grass:
  Shoes', trues', cert'nes sign ob rain!"
REFRAIN: "No, Brother Simmons, we kin safely say,
  'Tain't gwine tuh be no rain to-day,
  Kase da sut ain't fallin' an' da dogs ain't sleep,
  An' you ain't seen no spiders fum dare cobwebs creep;
  Las' night da sun went bright to bed,
  An' da moon ain't nevah once been seen to hang her head;
  If you'se watched all dis, den you kin safely say,
  Dat dare ain't a-gwine to be no rain to-day."

WAVERLEY TURNER CARMICHAEL

Keep Me, Jesus, Keep Me

Keep me 'neath Thy mighty wing,
Keep me, Jesus, keep me;
Help me praise Thy Holy name,
Keep me, Jesus, keep me.
O my Lamb, come, my Lamb,
O my good Lamb,
Save me, Jesus, save me.

Hear me as I cry to Thee;
Keep me, Jesus, keep me;
May I that bright glory see;
Keep me, Jesus, keep me.
O my Lamb, my good Lamb,
O my good Lamb,
Keep me, Jesus, keep me.

Winter Is Coming

De winter days are drawin' nigh
An' by the fire I sets an' sigh;
De nothe'n win' is blowin' cold,
Like it done in days of old.

De yaller leafs are fallin' fas',
Fur summer days is been an' pas';
The air is blowin' mighty cold,
Like it done in days of old.

De frost is fallin' on de gras'
An' seem to say "Dis is yo' las'"—
De air is blowin' mighty cold
Like it done in days of old.

ALICE DUNBAR-NELSON

SONNET

I had no thought of violets of late,
The wild, shy kind that spring beneath your feet
In wistful April days, when lovers mate
And wander through the fields in raptures sweet.
The thought of violets meant florists' shops,
And bows and pins, and perfumed papers fine;
And garish lights, and mincing little fops
And cabarets and songs, and deadening wine.
So far from sweet real things my thoughts had strayed,
I had forgot wide fields, and clear brown streams;
The perfect loveliness that God has made,—
Wild violets shy and Heaven-mounting dreams.
And now—unwittingly, you've made me dream
Of violets, and my soul's forgotten gleam.

CHARLES BERTRAM JOHNSON

A Little Cabin

Des a little cabin
Big ernuff fur two.
Des awaitin', honey,
Cozy fixt fur you;
Down dah by de road,
Not ve'y far from town,
Waitin' fur de missis,
When she's ready to come down.

Des a little cabin,
An' er acre o' groun',
Vines agrowin' on it,
Fruit trees all aroun',
Hollyhawks a-bloomin'
In de gyahden plot—
Honey, would you like to
Own dat little spot?

Make dat little cabin
Cheery, clean an' bright,
With an' angel in it
Like a ray of light?
Make dat little palace
Somethin' fine an' gran',
Make it like an Eden,
Fur a lonely man?

Des you listen, Honey,
While I 'splain it all,
How some lady's go'nter
Boss dat little hall;
Des you take my ban'
Dat's de way it's writ,
Des you take my heart,
Dat's de deed to it.

Negro Poets

Full many lift and sing
Their sweet imagining;
Not yet the Lyric Seer,
The one bard of the throng,
With highest gift of song,
Breaks on our sentient ear.

Not yet the gifted child,
With notes enraptured, wild,
That storm and throng the heart,
To make his rage our own,
Our hearts his lyric throne;
Hard won by cosmic art.

I hear the sad refrain,
Of slavery's sorrow-strain;
The broken half-lispt speech
Of freedom's twilit hour;
The greater growing reach
Of larger latent power.

Here and there a growing note
Swells from a conscious throat;
Thrilled with a message fraught
The pregnant hour is near;
We wait our Lyric Seer,
By whom our wills are caught.

Who makes our cause and wrong
The motif of his song;
Who sings our racial good,
Bestows us honor's place,
The cosmic brotherhood
Of genius—not of race.

CHARLES BERTRAM JOHNSON

Blind Homer, Greek or Jew,
Of fame's immortal few
Would still be deathless born;
Frail Dunbar, black or white,
In Fame's eternal light,
Would shine a Star of Morn.

An unhorizoned range,
Our hour of doubt and change,
Gives song a nightless day,
Whose pen with pregnant mirth
Will give our longings birth,
And point our souls the way?

OTTO LELAND BOHANAN

The Dawn's Awake!

The Dawn's awake!
  A flash of smoldering flame and fire
Ignites the East. Then, higher, higher,
    O'er all the sky so gray, forlorn,
    The torch of gold is borne.

The Dawn's awake!
  The dawn of a thousand dreams and thrills.
And music singing in the hills
    A paean of eternal spring
    Voices the new awakening.

The Dawn's awake!
  Whispers of pent-up harmonies,
With the mingled fragrance of the trees;
      Faint snatches of half-forgotten song—
    Fathers! torn and numb,—
      The boon of light we craved, awaited long,
    Has come, has come!

The Washer-Woman

A great swart cheek and the gleam of tears,
The flutter of hopes and the shadow of fears,
And all day long the rub and scrub
With only a breath betwixt tub and tub.
Fool! Thou hast toiled for fifty years
And what hast thou now but thy dusty tears?
In silence she rubbed. . . But her face I had seen,
Where the light of her soul fell shining and clean.

THEODORE HENRY SHACKELFORD

The Big Bell in Zion

Come, children, hear the joyful sound,
    Ding, Dong, Ding.
Go spread the glad news all around,
    Ding, Dong, Ding.
Chorus: Oh, the big bell's tollin' up in Zion,
    The big bell's tollin' up in Zion,
    The big bell's tollin' up in Zion,
      Ding, Dong, Ding.

I've been abused and tossed about,
    Ding, Dong, Ding.
But glory to the Lamb, I shout!
    Ding, Dong, Ding.

My bruthah jus' sent word to me,
    Ding, Dong, Ding.
That he'd done set his own self free.
    Ding, Dong, Ding.

Ole massa said he could not go,
    Ding, Dong, Ding.
But he's done reached Ohio sho'.
    Ding, Dong, Ding.

Ise gwine to be real nice an' meek,
    Ding, Dong, Ding.
Den I'll run away myself nex' week.
    Ding, Dong, Ding.
Chorus: Oh, the big bell's tollin' up in Zion,
    The big bell's tollin' up in Zion,
    The big bell's tollin' up in Zion,
      Ding, Dong Ding.

THEODORE HENRY SHACKELFORD

LUCIAN B. WATKINS

Star of Ethiopia

Out in the Night thou art the sun
Toward which thy soul-charmed children run,
    The faith-high height whereon they see
    The glory of their Day To Be—
The peace at last when all is done.

The night is dark but, one by one,
Thy signals, ever and anon,
    Smile beacon answers to their plea,
    Out in the Night.

Ah, Life! thy storms these cannot shun;
Give them a hope to rest upon,
    A dream to dream eternally,
    The strength of men who would be free
And win the battle race begun,
    Out in the Night!

LUCIAN B. WATKINS

Two Points of View

From this low-lying valley; Oh, how sweet
And cool and calm and great is life, I ween,
There on yon mountain-throne—that sun-gold crest!

From this uplifted, mighty mountain-seat:
How bright and still and warm and soft and green
Seems yon low lily-vale of peace and rest!

To Our Friends

We've kept the faith. Our souls' high dreams
    Untouched by bondage and its rod,
Burn on! and on! and on! It seems
    We shall have FRIENDS—while God is God!

BENJAMIN BRAWLEY

My Hero

(To Robert Gould Shaw)

Flushed with the hope of high desire,
    He buckled on his sword,
To dare the rampart ranged with fire,
    Or where the thunder roared;
Into the smoke and flame he went,
    For God's great cause to die—
A youth of heaven's element,
    The flower of chivalry.

This was the gallant faith, I trow,
    Of which the sages tell;
On such devotion long ago
    The benediction fell;
And never nobler martyr burned,
    Or braver hero died,
Than he who worldly honor spurned
    To serve the Crucified.

And Lancelot and Sir Bedivere
    May pass beyond the pale,
And wander over moor and mere
    To find the Holy Grail;

But ever yet the prize forsooth
    My hero holds in fee;
And he is Blameless Knight in truth,
    And Galahad to me.

CHAUCER

Gone are the sensuous stars, and manifold,
Clear sunbeams burst upon the front of night;
Ten thousand swords of azure and of gold
Give darkness to the dark and welcome light;
Across the night of ages strike the gleams,
And leading on the gilded host appears
An old man writing in a book of dreams,
And telling tales of lovers for the years;
Still Troilus hears a voice that whispers, Stay;
In Nature's garden what a mad rout sings!
Let's hear these motley pilgrims wile away
The tedious hours with stories of old things;
Or might some shining eagle claim
These lowly numbers for the House of Fame!

JOSHUA HENRY JONES, JR.

To a Skull

Ghastly, ghoulish, grinning skull,
Toothless, eyeless, hollow, dull,
Why your smirk and empty smile
As the hours away you wile?
Has the earth become such bore
That it pleases nevermore?
Whence your joy through sun and rain?
Is 't because of loss of pain?
Have you learned what men learn not
That earth's substance turns to rot?
After learning now you scan
Vain endeavors man by man?
Do you mind that you as they
Once was held by mystic sway;
Dreamed and struggled, hoped and prayed,
Lolled and with the minutes played?
Sighed for honors; battles planned;
Sipped of cups that wisdom banned
But would please the weak frail flesh;
Suffered, fell, 'rose, struggled fresh?
Now that you are but a skull
Glimpse you life as life is, full
Of beauties that we miss
Till time withers with his kiss?
Do you laugh in cynic vein
Since you cannot try again?
And you know that we, like you,
Will too late our failings rue?
Tell me, ghoulish, grinning skull
What deep broodings, o'er you mull?
Tell me why you smirk and smile
Ere I pass life's sunset stile.

APPENDIX
PLÁCIDO'S SONNET TO HIS MOTHER

DESPIDA A MI MADRE

(En La Capilla)

Si la suerte fatal que me ha cabido,
Y el triste fin de mi sangrienta historia,
Al salir de esta vida transitoria
Deja tu corazon de muerte herido;
    Baste de Ilanto: el ánimo afligido
Recobre su quietud; moro en la gloria,
Y mi plácida lira á tu memoria
Lanza en la tumba su postrer sonido.

    Sonido dulce, melodioso y santo,
Glorioso, espiritual, puro y divino,
Inocente, espontáneo como el llanto
    Que vertiera al nacer: ya el cuello inclino!
Ya de la religion me cubre el manto!
Adios, mi madre! adios—El Peligrino.

Farewell to My Mother

(In the Chapel)

The appointed lot has come upon me, mother,
The mournful ending of my years of strife,
This changing world I leave, and to another
In blood and terror goes my spirit's life.
But thou, grief-smitten, cease thy mortal weeping
And let thy soul her wonted peace regain;
I fall for right, and thoughts of thee are sweeping
Across my lyre to wake its dying strains.
A strain of joy and gladness, free, unfailing
All glorious and holy, pure, divine,
And innocent, unconscious as the wailing
I uttered on my birth; and I resign
Even now, my life, even now descending slowly,
Faith's mantle folds me to my slumbers holy.
Mother, farewell! God keep thee—and forever!

Translated by William Cullen Bryant.

Plácido's Farewell to his Mother

*(Written in the Chapel of the Hospital de Santa Cristina
on the Night Before His Execution)*

If the unfortunate fate engulfing me,
The ending of my history of grief,
The closing of my span of years so brief,
Mother, should wake a single pang in thee,
Weep not. No saddening thought to me devote;
I calmly go to a death that is glory-filled,
My lyre before it is forever stilled
Breathes out to thee its last and dying note.

A note scarce more than a burden-easing sigh,
Tender and sacred, innocent, sincere—
Spontaneous and instinctive as the cry
I gave at birth—And now the hour is here—
O God, thy mantle of mercy o'er my sins!
Mother, farewell! The pilgrimage begins.

Translated by James Weldon Johnson.

Biographical Index of Authors

Bohanan, Otto Leland. Born in Washington, D.C. Educated in the public schools in Washington. He is a graduate of Howard University, School of Liberal Arts, Washington, D.C., and did special work in English at the Catholic University in that city. At present he is engaged in the musical profession in New York.

Braithwaite, William Stanley. Born in Boston, 1878. Mainly self-educated. A critic of poetry and the friend of poets. Author of *Lyrics-of Life, The House of Falling Leaves, The Poetic Year, The Story of the Great War,* etc. Editor and compiler of *The Book of Elizabethan Verse, The Book of Georgian Verse, The Book of Restoration Verse* and a series of yearly anthologies of magazine verse. One of the literary editors of the Boston *Transcript*.

Brawley, Benjamin. Born at Columbia, S.C., 1882. Educated at the Atlanta Baptist College, the University of Chicago and Harvard University. For two years he was professor of English at Howard University, Washington, D.C. Later he became dean of Morehouse College, Atlanta, Ga. Author of *A Short History of the American Negro, The Negro in Literature and Art, A Short History of the English Drama, A Social History of the American Negro*, etc. Now living in Boston and engaged in research and writing.

Campbell, James Edwin. Was born at Pomeroy, Ohio, in the early sixties. His early life was somewhat shrouded in mystery; he never referred to it even to his closest associates. He was educated in the public schools of his native city. Later he spent a while at Miami College. In the late eighties and early nineties he was engaged in newspaper work in Chicago. He wrote regularly on the various dailies of that city. He was also one of a group that issued the *Four O'Clock Magazine*, a literary publication which flourished for several years. He died, perhaps, twenty years ago. He was the author of *Echoes from The Cabin and Elsewhere*, a volume of poems.

Carmichael, Waverley Turner. A young man who had never been out of his native state of Alabama until several years ago when he entered one of the summer courses at Harvard University. His education to that time had been very limited and he had endured poverty and hard work. His verses came to the attention of one of the Harvard professors. He has since published a volume, *From the Heart of a Folk*. He served with the 367th Regiment, "The Buffaloes," during the World War and saw active service in France. At present he is employed as a postal clerk in Boston, Mass.

CORROTHERS, JAMES D., 1869–1919. Born in Cass County, Michigan. Student in Northwestern University, minister and poet. Many of his poems appeared in *The Century Magazine*.

COTTER, JOSEPH S., JR., 1895–1919. Born at Louisville, Kentucky, in the room in which Paul Laurence Dunbar first read his dialect poems in the South. He was precocious as a child, having read a number of books before he was six years old. All through his boyhood he had the advantage and inspiration of the full library of poetic books belonging to his father, himself a poet of considerable talent. Young Cotter attended Fisk University but left in his second year because he had developed tuberculosis. A volume of verse, *The Band of Gideon*, and a number of unpublished poems were written during the six years in which he was an invalid.

DANDRIDGE, RAY G. Born at Cincinnati, Ohio, 1882. Educated in the grammar and high school of his native city. In 1912, as the result of illness, he lost the use of both legs and his right arm. He does most of his writing lying flat in bed and using his left hand. He is the author of *The Poet and Other Poems*.

DAVIS, DANIEL WEBSTER. Born in Virginia, near Richmond. For a number of years he was a minister and principal of the largest public school in Richmond. He died in that city some years ago. He was the author of '*Weh Down Souf*, a volume of verse. He was very popular as an orator and a reader of his own poems.

DETT, R. NATHANIEL. Born at Drummondville, Canada, 1882. Graduate of the Oberlin Conservatory of Music. He is a composer, most of his compositions being based on themes from the old "slave songs." His "Listen to de Lambs" is widely used by choral societies. He is director of music at Hampton Institute. He is also the author of *The Album of a Heart*, a volume of verse.

Du Bois, W. E. Burghardt. Born at Great Barrington, Mass., 1868. Educated at Fisk University, Harvard University and the University of Berlin. For a number of years professor of economics and history at Atlanta University. Author of the *Suppression of the Slave Trade, The Philadelphia Negro, The Souls of Black Folk, John Brown, Darkwater*, etc. He is the editor of *The Crisis*.

Dunbar, Paul Laurence. Born at Dayton, Ohio, 1872; died 1906. Dunbar was educated in the public schools. He wrote his early poems while working as an elevator boy. His first volume of poems, *Oak and Ivy*, was published in 1893 and sold largely through his own efforts. This was followed by *Majors and Minors, Lyrics of Lowly Life, Lyrics of the Hearthside, Lyrics of Love and Laughter, Lyrics of Sunshine and Shadow* and *Howdy, Honey, Howdy. Lyrics of Lowly Life*, published in New York in 1896 with an introduction written by William Dean Howells, gained national recognition for Dunbar. In addition to poetical works, Dunbar was the author of four novels, *The Uncalled, The Love of Landry, The Sport of the Gods*, and *The Fanatics*. He also published several volumes of short stories. Partly because of his magnificent voice and refined manners, he was a very successful reader of his own poems and was able to add greatly to their popularity.

Fauset, Jessie Redmon. Born at Snow Hill, New Jersey. She was educated in the public schools of Philadelphia, at Cornell University and the University of Pennsylvania. For a while she was teacher of French in the Dunbar High School, Washington, D.C. Author of a number of uncollected poems and several short stories. She is literary editor of *The Crisis*.

Hill, Leslie Pinckney. Born at Lynchburg, Va., 1880. He was educated in the public schools at Lynchburg and at Harvard University. On graduation he became a teacher of English and methods at Tuskegee. Author of the *Wings of Oppression*, a volume of verse. He is principal of the Cheyney Training School for Teachers at Cheyney, Pa.

Holloway, John Wesley. Born in Merriweather County, Ga, 1865. His father, who learned to read and write in slavery, became one of the first colored teachers in Georgia after the Civil War. Mr. Holloway was educated at Clark University, Atlanta, Ga., and at Fisk University,

Nashville, Tenn. He was for a while a member of the Fisk Jubilee Singers. Has been a teacher and is now a preacher. He is the author of *From the Desert*, a volume of verse.

JAMISON, ROSCOE C. Born at Winchester, Tenn., 1888; died 1918. He was a graduate of Fisk University.

JOHNSON, CHARLES BERTRAM. Born at Callao, Mo., 1880. He was educated in the public schools of his home town and at Western College, Lincoln Institute and at Chicago University. He was a teacher for a number of years and is now a pastor of a church at Moberly, Mo. He is the author of *Songs of My People*.

JOHNSON, FENTON. Born at Chicago, 1888. He was educated in the public schools and at the University of Chicago and Northwestern University. The author of *A Little Dreaming, Songs of the Soil* and *Visions of the Dusk*. He has devoted much time to journalism and the editing of a magazine.

JOHNSON, GEORGIA DOUGLAS. Born in Atlanta, Ga., 1886. She was educated in the public schools of that city and at Atlanta University. She is the author of a volume of verse, *The Heart of a Woman* and other poems.

JOHNSON, JAMES WELDON. Born at Jacksonville, Fla., 1871. He was educated in the public schools of Jacksonville, at Atlanta University and at Columbia University. He taught school in his native town for several years. Later he came to New York with his brother, J. Rosamond Johnson, and began writing for the musical comedy stage. He served seven years as U. S. Consul in Venezuela and Nicaragua. Author of *The Autobiography of an Ex-colored Man, Fifty Years and Other Poems*, and the English libretto to *Goyescas*, the Spanish grand opera, produced at the Metropolitan Opera House in 1915.

JONES, EDWARD SMYTH. Attracted national attention about ten years ago by walking some hunderds of miles from his home in the South to Harvard University. Arriving there, he was arrested on a charge of vagrancy. While in jail, he wrote a poem, "Harvard Square." The poem created a sentiment that led to his quick release. He is the author of *The Sylvan Cabin*.

JONES, JOSHUA HENRY, JR. He is engaged in newspaper work in Boston and is the author of a volume of poems, *The Heart of the World*.

MARGETSON, GEORGE REGINALD. Was born at St. Kitts, British West Indies, in 1877. He was educated at the Moravian school in his district. He came to the United States in 1897. Mr. Margetson has found it necessary to work hard to support a large family and his poems have been written in his spare moments. He is the author of two volumes of verses, *Songs of Life* and *The Fledgling Bard and the Poetry Society* and, in addition, a large number of uncollected poems. Mr. Margetson lives in Boston.

McCLELLAN, GEORGE MARION. Born at Belfast, Tenn., 1860. Graduate of Fisk University and Hartford Theological Seminary, teacher, principal and author. He is the author of *The Path of Dreams*.

McKAY, CLAUDE. Born in Jamaica, West Indies, 1889. Such education as he gained in boyhood he received from his brother. He served for a while as a member of the Kingston Constabulary. In 1912 he came to the United States. For two years he was a student of agriculture at the Kansas State College. Since leaving school Mr. McKay has turned his hand to any kind of work to earn a living. He has worked in hotels and on the Pullman cars. He is to-day associate editor of *The Liberator*. He is the author of two volumes of poems, *Songs of Jamaica* and *Spring in New Hampshire*, the former published in Jamaica and the latter in London.

MOORE; WILLIAM H. A. Was born in New York City and received his education in the public schools and at the City College. He also did some special work at Columbia University. He has had a long career as a newspaper man, working on both white and colored publications. He now lives in Chicago. He is the author of *Dusk Songs*, a volume of poems.

NELSON, ALICE MOORE (DUNBAR). Born at New Orleans, La., 1875. She was educated in the schools of New Orleans and has taken special courses at Cornell University, Columbia University, and the University of Pennsylvania. Author of *Violets and Other Tales, The Goodness of St. Rocque, Masterpieces of Negro Eloquence*, and *The Dunbar Speaker*. She was married to Paul Laurence Dunbar in 1898. She has been a teacher and is well known on the lecture platform and as an editor.

ROGERS, ALEX. Born at Nashville, Tenn., 1876. Educated in the public schools of that city. For many years a writer of words for popular songs. He wrote many of the songs for the musical comedies in which Williams and Walker appeared. He is the author of *The Jonah Man, Nobody* and other songs made popular by Mr. Bert Williams.

SHACKELFORD, THEODORE HENRY. Author of *Mammy's Cracklin' Bread and Other Poems*, and *My Country and Other Poems*.

SPENCER, ANNE. Born in Bramwell, W. Va., 1882. Educated at the Virginia Seminary, Lynchburg, Va. She lives at Lynchburg and takes great pride and pleasure in her garden.

WATKINS, LUCIAN B., was born in Virginia. He served overseas in the great war and lost his health. He died in 1921. He was the author of a large number of uncollected poems.

A Note About the Author

James Weldon Johnson (1871–1938) was an African American writer and civil rights activist. Born in Jacksonville, Florida, he obtained an education from a young age, first by his mother, a musician and teacher, and then at the Edwin M. Stanton School. In 1894, he graduated from Atlanta University, a historically Black college known for its rigorous classical curriculum. With his brother Rosamond, he moved to New York City, where they excelled as songwriters for Broadway. His poem "Lift Ev'ry Voice and Sing" (1899), set to music by Rosamond, eventually became known as the "Negro National Anthem." Over the next several decades, he dedicated himself to education, activism, and diplomacy. From 1906 to 1913, he worked as a United States Consul, first in Puerto Cabello, Venezuela, and then in Nicaragua. He married Grace Nail, an activist and artist, in 1910, and would return to New York with her following the end of his diplomatic career. While in Nicaragua, he wrote and anonymously published *The Autobiography of an Ex-Colored Man* (1912), a novel exploring the phenomenon of racial passing. In 1917, Johnson began his work with the NAACP, eventually rising to the role of executive secretary. He became known as a towering figure of the Harlem Renaissance, writing poems and novels as well as compiling such anthologies as *The Book of American Negro Poetry* (1922). For his contributions to African American culture as an artist and patron, his activism against lynching, and his pioneering work as the first African American professor at New York University, Johnson is considered one of twentieth century America's leading cultural figures.

A Note from the Publisher

Spanning many genres, from non-fiction essays to literature classics to children's books and lyric poetry, Mint Edition books showcase the master works of our time in a modern new package. The text is freshly typeset, is clean and easy to read, and features a new note about the author in each volume. Many books also include exclusive new introductory material. Every book boasts a striking new cover, which makes it as appropriate for collecting as it is for gift giving. Mint Edition books are only printed when a reader orders them, so natural resources are not wasted. We're proud that our books are never manufactured in excess and exist only in the exact quantity they need to be read and enjoyed.

Discover more of your favorite classics with Bookfinity™.

- Track your reading with custom book lists.
- Get great book recommendations for your personalized Reader Type.
- Add reviews for your favorite books.
- AND MUCH MORE!

Visit **bookfinity.com** and take the fun Reader Type quiz to get started.

Enjoy our classic and modern companion pairings!